PNW   Cross, Mary Bywater,
746.97 1942-   Keep '09
CRO   Treasures in the
c.2   trunk $24.95
       √6/23 KBK NOV 27 1995
       √ Keep 11/13 table

Keep '09

DATE DUE

DEC 12 1995			
RC-EE JUL 09 '03			
GAYLORD			PRINTED IN U.S.A.

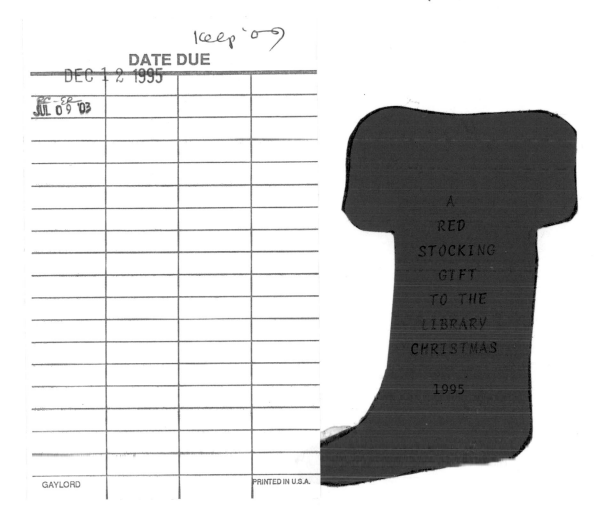

A
RED
STOCKING
GIFT
TO THE
LIBRARY
CHRISTMAS

1995

P9-CIU-201

TREASURES IN THE TRUNK

TREASURES IN THE TRUNK

Quilts of the Oregon Trail

Mary Bywater Cross

RUTLEDGE HILL PRESS
NASHVILLE, TENNESSEE

To the memory of my grandmother
Harriet Louisa Smith McNeill
1887–1976

Copyright © 1993 by Mary Bywater Cross

All rights reserved. Written permission must be secured from the publisher to use or reproduce any part of this book, except for brief quotations in critical reviews or articles.

Published in Nashville, Tennessee, by Rutledge Hill Press, Inc.,
211 Seventh Avenue North, Nashville, Tennessee 37219.
Distributed in Canada by H. B. Fenn & Company, Ltd., Mississauga, Ontario.

Design by Harriette Bateman
Typography by D&T/Bailey, Nashville, Tennessee

Library of Congress Cataloging-in-Publication Data

Cross, Mary Bywater, 1942–
      Treasures in the trunk : quilts of the Oregon Trail / Mary Bywater
Cross.
          p.   cm.
      Includes bibliographical references and index.
      ISBN 1-55853-219-6   — ISBN 1-55853-237-4 (pbk.)
      1. Quilts—Oregon Trail—History—19th century—Catalogs.
   2. Quiltmakers—Oregon Trail—Biography.   I. Title.
   NK9112.C76   1993
   746.9'7'0973—dc20   92-45831
                                                                                   CIP

Printed in Hong Kong
3 4 5 6 — 97 96 95 94 93

PNW
746.97

CR D.
C.1   Red Sth 9 4

PNW   BT   2495   11-17-94

CONTENTS

An estimated 300,000 pioneers traveled the Oregon Trail by wagon train.

PREFACE

Between 1840 and 1870, a quarter of a million Americans crossed the continent to Oregon and California in what was considered one of the great migrations of modern times. Since the year 1993 marks the 150th anniversary of the first wagon train into Oregon, the event is being observed by major celebrations throughout the West, especially in Oregon.

The settling of the West has long been portrayed through the visual arts in paintings, films, photographs, and drawings; and innumerable books, journals, diaries, and letters have been written about the experience. Many of these were contributed by men and therefore represent a male perspective. At the time they were written, these contributions were important resources to describe the physical characteristics of the landscape and the encounters with Indians, traders, and animals. In general they gave recommendations to others planning to explore the West.

Popular literature of the period 1840–1875 featured the adventures of such heroes as Davy Crockett and Daniel Boone foraging and fighting to lead the settlement effort. Focusing on the Oregon experience were men like Francis Parkman, author of *The Oregon Trail*; William Henry Jackson, watercolor artist of a freight-wagon train whose works are housed at the Scott's Bluff National Monument in Gering, Nebraska; and Ezra Meeker, the only pioneer to cover the route by wagon, train, automobile, and airplane. Their works did much to promote the idea of going to Oregon and to educate the public about the experience.

At the same time, the female perspective was ignored or avoided. With an increased focus on women's history, contemporary contributions have been made to understand the Westward Movement from their point of view. Works by Julie Roy Jeffrey, Sandra Myres, and Lillian Schlissel, through their studies of literate American women's recorded documents—diaries, letters, journals, and books—have been major resources for this long-overdue emphasis.

Jeffrey, in her book *Frontier Women, The Trans-Mississippi West 1840–1880*, examines how nineteenth-century American society's definition of women as agents of civilization and keepers of morals was challenged by the experience of living on the frontier. Working from the long-established but challenged thesis of Frederick Jackson Turner that as Americans moved West the new environment gradually weakened inherited culture and forced them to create new institutions and values, Jeffrey concluded that women held to society's definition of their role and were proud of their contributions of creating social and educational institutions for their families and communities.

The focus of Sandra Myres's *Westering Women and the Frontier Experience 1800–1915* was to identify women's place within the context of the American frontier by reviewing the preconceptions about the experience held by men and women and to see how they were changed by participation in it.

Lillian Schlissel, in *Women's Diaries of the Westward Journey*, uses her study of 103 different white women's writings to reconstruct the daily lives of these women in an effort to define their role in the Westward Movement. A goal of her work was to understand the design of the emigrant family and to see its dimensions of emotional balance and work roles.

According to Schlissel, women went West because there was no way for them *not* to go once the decision was made by their husbands and fathers, whom they were committed to support. She concluded:

> The period of the overland trail migration (1840–1860) produces overwhelming evidence that women did not greet the idea of going West with enthusiasm, but rather that they worked out a painful negotiation with historical imperatives and personal necessity.[1]

Within cycles of childbearing and childrearing, women managed a kind of equity in which to place their lives. They were neither brave adventurers nor sunbonneted weepers. They were vigorous and given to realism and stoicism. To them the West meant the challenge of rearing a family and maintaining domestic order within the disordered life on the frontier. Once embarked on the journey, they were determined and energetic in their efforts to make the move a success.[2]

In a detailed study of four families in *Far from Home, Families of the Westward Journey*, Lillian Schlissel, Byrd Gibbens, and Elizabeth Hampsten present evidence of how the frontiers in general affected their subjects' lives as humans and as families. The events and activities on the journey definitely changed the lives of the participants. With eagerness and enthusiasm, the families agreed to undertake their journeys, then later helplessly watched as disasters and complications overwhelmed them.

Finally, at their destinations the families were forced to make changes in order to survive. The despair and emotional destruction forced on them by the geographic isolation of the families, due to the frontier distances, brought on a yearning for the place they had started from. Some were able to return home. Others maintained a connection with family and friends left behind, constantly writing to request photographs, seeds, and scraps of clothing.[3] These scraps often went into the quilts that became the *Treasures in the Trunk,* to be celebrated and caressed and used to stir the memories of those "back in the States."

Because the focus of this book is on quilts as products of needlework skills, I studied the role of needlework within the framework of the nineteenth-century woman's life. This has coincided with quilt historians who have been gathering data about quilts that were made in America over the last two hundred years.

Barbara Brackman's books, *Clues in the Calico* and *Encyclopedia of Pieced Quilt Patterns,* have been extremely helpful in attempting to date the quilts and identify pattern sources. Most of this work has been done within the framework of state quilt projects that have recorded the history of quilts made within politically and geographically defined borders. More often than not, the quilts reflect the static aspect of American society, quilts made by women who stayed home and later were kept at home by the children who chose to remain there. These projects have analyzed regional trends, individual styles, ethnic group quilts, and industrial influences. State project publications as complete as *Quilts in Community: Ohio's Traditions* by Ricky Clark, George Knepper, and Ellice Ronsheim have been an important resource to this study because many of the cross-country emigrants originally came from that midwestern region.

These studies have shown that women used their needles to make quilts that reflected the passages in their lives. Studies from state documentation projects and museum exhibitions have yielded information showing that quilts were produced for the major events of birth, childhood, coming of age, marriage, death, and involvement in church and community activities. The coming of age passage has shown a general group of quilts related to becoming an adult, to serving in the military, and to taking leave of home.

This book differs from many others in that it is the first to look at quilts made in an extended span of time and sweep of distance. It looks at the quilts and at the women who made them, and considers quilts in three categories: those made before the journey, those made during the journey, and those made afterward, covering the period from 1825 to 1915. The quilts are presented chronologically within three definite periods when the women or families connected to the quilts made the journey: 1840–50, 1851–55, and 1856–70. These periods are defined by the conditions that influenced and affected the migration. The quilts were often started in one location and completed in another far distant, separated by more than two thousand miles' distance and six months' time.

Treasures in the Trunk presents quilts as documents of history, similar to diaries, in order to learn about the lives of the women who made the migration. To be considered valid documents of history, according to textile historian Rachel Maines, quilts must meet necessary requirements: they must have a continuous and traceable history; they must reflect the experience of the mainstream; and they must be honest in representing the free expression of the maker.[4]

I have sought to validate the quilts included here by their connection to the family, the maker, and the Oregon Trail experience in terms of when they were made, by whom, and the years the families crossed the plains. The documentation on the makers includes the dates of their lives, their birth and settlement locations, and information about their husbands and families. If it was available, additional material is included about the role each played in the settlement of the Northwest.

The findings are the result of studying seventy quilts and their makers from 1825 to 1915, quilts found today in national and western public and private collections. Then, using the thesis work of Professor Christopher Carlson entitled *The Rural Family in the 19th Century: A Case Study in Oregon's Willamette Valley,* I attempted to infer how the quilts celebrated the lives of the quiltmakers.

For this project, I have numbered the quilts chronologically by when they were made. References to specific quilts are by maker or family name and assigned number. A chart of all quilts is in Appendix A.

My major research directives have been: what are the quilts; who were the makers; how do these quilts reflect the lives of these westering women; where are the quilts located; and how were they used on the Trail and in the homes?

My conclusions are drawn from the study of the quilts as a body of work done within each maker's lifetime. Looking for common patterns, fabrics, quilting motifs, and styles, I sought to identify themes of nature, movement, friendship, and celebration, all related to the common overall theme of migration.

ACKNOWLEDGMENTS

THREE YEARS AGO I BEGAN SHAPING PLANS for a quilt project related to the Oregon Trail. The first stage of the project was an informed search for the quilts, which also helped define the scope of the project. This search could not have been undertaken without the interest and support of institutions, quilt documentation projects, and individuals throughout the country, particularly in the Northwest. This interest was sparked by the scheduled celebration of the 150th anniversary of the first wagon train over the Oregon Trail in 1843, and the support stemmed from the recognition of quilts' value as cultural artifacts of women's history. Many responded to my first survey inquiry while others gladly opened their storage and records for follow-up research. I extend my appreciation to all who helped.

I first want to acknowledge Jim Renner, interpretative director of the Oregon Trail Coordinating Council and the initial person assigned the task to develop the celebration, who was involved from the beginning. Through him I came in contact with Daniel Robertson, director of the Douglas County Museum of History and Natural History, who co-directed the survey and research phases in preparation for the traveling exhibit sponsored by the museum. This partnership enabled funding from the Oregon Council for the Humanities and the Friends of the Douglas County Museum of History and Natural History to support my work and create a higher level of acceptance of it.

Later, a fellowship from the Oregon Council for the Humanities to attend the National Endowment for the Humanities Research Conference, "A New Significance: Re-Envisioning the History of the American West," helped to shape my findings and focus my conclusions.

For the book phase I am greatly indebted to Joyce Ruff Abdill, Chair of the Douglas County Museum Advisory Committee and publisher's representative for Rutledge Hill Press, who knew there would be interest in the book and promoted the idea with Ron Pitkin and Larry Stone of Rutledge Hill Press. I am also indebted to Bets Ramsey, quilt book editor at Rutledge Hill Press, for her enthusiasm and support from the beginning, which greatly helped to bring the concept for the book to reality.

Responses to the survey of more than one hundred institutions

PHOTO CREDITS

Photographs are credited to the following: Bill Bachhuber, xiv, xv, xvi, 10, 11, 12, 13, 14, 15, 16, 17, 18, 19, 20, 21, 22, 23, 27, 30, 31, 32, 33, 48, 49, 58, 59, 61, 64, 65, 66, 67, 68, 69, 70, 71, 72, 73, 80, 81, 82, 83, 100, 101, 104, 105, 106, 107, 108, 109, 112, 113, 118, 119, 157, 160; Jack Liu, 8, 9, 24, 25, 26, 34, 35, 52, 53, 54, 55, 62, 63, 74, 75, 88, 89, 114, 115; George Champlin, 28, 29, 46, 47, 50, 51, 61, 84, 85, 110, 111; Charlotte Pendleton, 11; Matt Strieby, 56, 57, 60, 87, 102, 103, 117, 126; David Anderson, 76, 77; Mark Gulezian, 79

PHOTO PERMISSIONS

Grateful acknowledgment is hereby given to the following owners who have graciously given permission to reproduce their quilts and photographs: Smith-Western, Inc., Portland, Oregon, vi; National Park Service, Scotts Bluff National Monument, Gering, Nebraska, xviii–1, 36–37, 90–91, 120–121, 127; collection of the author, xiv, xv, xvi; Oregon Historical Society, Portland, Oregon, xvii (Neg #83930), 5 (Neg #55094), 7 (Neg #5997), 28, 29, 46 (Neg # 017763), 47, 50, 51, 62 (Neg #11017), 63, 84 (Neg #13641), 85, 95 (Neg #61320), 110, 111, 128 (Neg #4601), 129 (Neg #770), 130 (Neg #38005), 13 (Neg

#56235), 132 (Neg #11054); Oregon State Society of the Daughters of the American Revolution Pioneer Mothers Cabin, St. Paul, Oregon, 5; Lane County Historical Museum, Eugene, Oregon, 6, 8, 9, 34, 35, 52, 53, 74, 75, 88, 89, 114, 115; Yamhill County Museum, Lafayette, Oregon, 10, 82, 83; Oregon State Society of the Daughters of the American Revolution Schminck Museum, Lakeview, Oregon, 11, 12, 13, 14, 15, 16, 17, 18, 19, 20, 21, 22, 23, 44; Horner Museum, Corvallis, Oregon, 24, 25; JoAnn Wiss, 24; Molalla Area Historical Society, Molalla, Oregon, 27, 64, 65, 70, 71, 80, 81; Bertha Nolan, 26; Louise Godfrey, 30, 31; Douglas County Museum of History and Natural History, Roseburg, Oregon, 32, 58, 59; John and Carol Herman, 33; Patricia Erlandson, 48, 49, Lincoln County Historical Society, Newport, Oregon, 54, 55; Southern Oregon Historical Society, Medford, Oregon, 56 (Neg #5682), 57, 60, 86 (Neg #14057), 87, 102, 103, 116 (Neg #1805), 117, 125 (Neg #403), 126; Lois Ann Stewart, 61, 157, 160; Leona Donaldson Rink and Honora Dallas, 64, 65; Aurora Colony Historical Society, Aurora, Oregon, 72, 73, 118, 119; Cheney Cowles Museum/Eastern Washington Historical Society, Spokane, Washington, 76, 77; Oregon/Idaho Conference United Methodist Archives, Williamette University, Salem, Oregon, 77; Kentucky Department of Parks, William Whitley State Historic Site, Sanford, Kentucky, 78; Daughters of the American Revolution Museum, Washington, D.C., Gift of Linn Chapter, Oregon State Society (Photo courtesy of the Oregon State Society), 79; Vera Kocher Yoder, 100, 101; Donald and Gilberta Lieuallen, 104, 105, 106, 107, 108, 109; Helen Barrett Woodroofe, 112, 113; Museum of American History, Smithsonian Institution, Washington, D.C., 123, 124; Deborah Bell Blaedel, 123; Pacific University Museum, Forest Grove, Oregon, 143.

and quilt projects shaped my travel itinerary and led me to the quilts. These also provided much of the information described in Appendix B about preserving quilted treasures.

Locally, the following Oregon county museums and historical societies participated: Douglas County; Lane County; Yamhill County; Lincoln County; Polk County; Benton County; Clackamas County; Klamath County; Coos County; Washington County; Crook County; Umatilla County; and Linn County.

These Oregon regional historical societies also participated: Molalla Area; Junction City; Southern Oregon in Medford; and the Oregon Historical Society in Portland. Oregon regional museums included: Old Aurora Colony Society in Aurora; Horner Museum at Oregon State University in Corvallis; High Desert Museum in Bend; McLoughlin House National Historic Site in Oregon City; Pacific University Museum in Forest Grove; Archives of the Oregon/Idaho Conference of the First United Methodist Church at Willamette University in Salem; and the four museums owned and operated by the Oregon State Society of the Daughters of the American Revolution, Schminck Memorial Museum in Lakeview, Pioneer Mothers Cabin and Robert Newell House at St. Paul, and Caples House Museum at Columbia City.

The following Washington historical museums and sites participated: Cheney Cowles Museum/Eastern Washington Historical Society in Spokane; Fort Walla Walla; Whitman Mission; Lewis County; Thurston County Historic Commission; and the Museum of History and Industry in Seattle.

On the national level, the institutions that provided access to their resources either through direct use of their libraries or by computer link-up were the Library of Congress, the National Museum of American History of the Smithsonian Institution, the Daughters of the American Revolution Museum, all in Washington, D.C.; the New England Historical and Genealogical Society in Boston; and the Family History Centers and International Genealogical Index of the Church of Christ of Latter Day Saints based in Salt Lake City. These resources provided the valuable family materials to validate and enrich my research.

Following my initial quilt research, many individuals answered questions, provided key leads, and assisted with the project. Some were part of the volunteer or small professional staffs of the societies already mentioned, while others were family members or owners of quilts or personal friends interested in the project. The list is long, but each person is deserving of mention. I hope I have not omitted anyone from the list.

The owners of Oregon Trail quilts were Deborah Bell Blaedel, Vera Yoder, Patricia Erlandson, Leona Donaldson Rink, Honora Dallas, Louise Godfrey, John and Carol Herman, Wanita Propst

Haugen, Donald and Gilberta Lieuallen, Helen Woodroofe, Lois Stewart, and JoAnn Wiss.

The professionals and volunteers were Deborah Confer, Marty West, Janette Merriman, Steve Wyatt, Nancy Tuckhorn, Barb Abrams, Marsha Matthews, Sieglinde Smith, Irene Zenev, Laura Thayer, Patrick Harris, Loretta Harrison, Marilen Poole, Dick Ackerman, Jean Shaw, Mary Jane Hendricks, Dorothy West, Richard Read, Brooks Howard, Karen Fox, Joyce White, Gerry Frank, Robert Monaghan, Joan Kelley, Shannon Applegate, Eileen Fitzsimmons, Nancy Russell, Marilyn Deering, Kelly Allen, Sue Morelang, Mary Dorsett, Mabry Benson, Susan Butruille, Bertha Nolan, Lida Childers, Bonnie Furry, Frederick Scoggin, Jack Liu, George Champlin, Mark Strieby, and Christopher Carlson.

The San Francisco-based American Quilt Study Group's network of quilt historians and researchers proved a valuable resource. Particularly helpful was correspondence from Nancy Tuckhorn, Carolyn Davis, Mary Alma Parker, Virginia Gunn, Suellen Meyer, Elly Sienkiewicz, Bets Ramsey, Ricky Clark, and Barbara Brackman.

Those special people who went beyond reasonable expectations to provide information and support were Ricky Clark, Charlotte Pendleton, Ruth Stoller, Gena Cline, Katherine Johnson, Ellen Benedict, Virginia Burgh, Jane Pubols, Sandra Thirtyacre, Barbara Lund, Shannon and Kent Madison, Bill Bachhuber, and Nancy Stuckey. Unique and special was the unfailing guidance and support of Bob Burco who showed me how to access and use my resources and edited early drafts of the manuscript.

Finally, I acknowledge my debt for the personal support of family and friends across the country as I sought to create a meaningful contribution to the celebration of the 150th anniversary of the Oregon Trail through the legacy of quilts and their makers. I owe you all my grateful thanks.

NOTE

The quilts of this book reflect their historical significance as cultural artifacts and focus on the lives of the women who made them. In many cases, the quilts were needed and used by their owners. In that respect each has unique value and heritage, regardless of its physical condition. The intent of the photographs has been to record each quilt as an important historical item and not solely as an antique destined to awe the viewer with its beauty and craftsmanship. The subject is both women's history and quilt history.

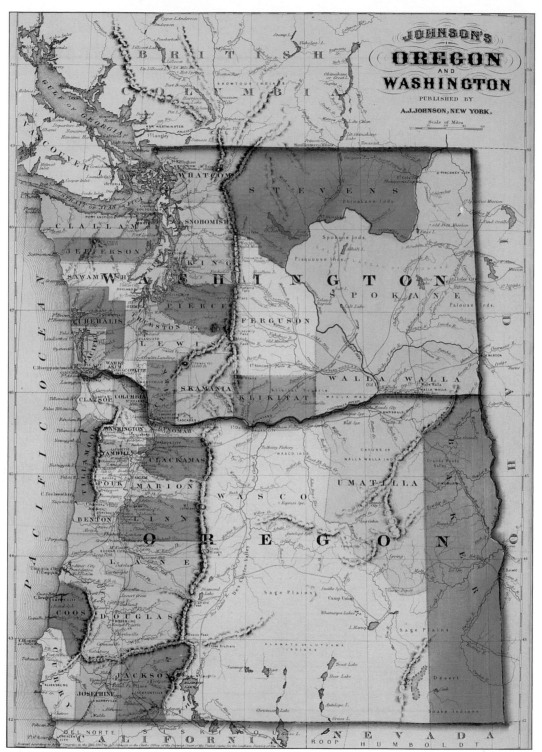

Counties in Oregon and Washington where Oregon Trail pioneers settled, circa 1865

INTRODUCTION

The gay colored quilts which came across in a big chest, and which had been used as wrapping for a few cherished dishes and other treasures, were unpacked. . . . Other bits from the old home three thousand miles away were placed on the crude shelves; a picture of Grandmother's parents; a few books, the family Bible, the little treasures which had been slipped between the bedding in an old chest and a queer looking trunk lined with bright flowered paper. They were now at home.[1]

AND SO IT WAS, AS THOUSANDS OF WOMEN arrived in the Northwest by way of the Oregon Trail. This migration or "leave-taking" would consume the longest time and widest distance for these nineteenth-century women to establish new homes for themselves and their loved ones.

The Women

All would begin the journey with individual life experiences that varied according to their ages, stages in personal relationships, societal background, and expectations. Slowly covering the distance at a rate of five to twenty miles a day, from four to nine months, each woman would experience a personal transition, whether physically, emotionally, mentally, socially, or culturally.

All challenges—pregnancy, illness, death of loved ones, exhaustion, isolation, cultural identity, and moral beliefs—were to be confronted in an unknown world far from their original homes. This experience would have a major impact on their lives, changing their views, expectations, and accomplishments.

A major factor in how they reacted to and interpreted their trail experience would be their educational background. For the nineteenth-century daughter lucky enough to have formal educa-

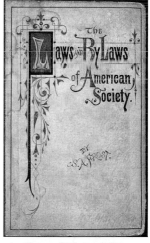

Cover of nineteenth-century etiquette book

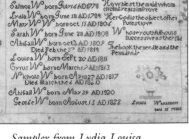

Sampler from Lydia Louisa
Whittemore Hutchins, 1811–1892

tion, it would be defined as the following sampler verse stitched by my great, great grandmother Lydia Louisa Whittemore Hutchins in 1824 in Massachusetts:

> How blest the maid whom circling years improve
> Her God is the object of her warmest love
> Whose youthful hours successive as they glide
> The book, the Needle, and the Pen divide.[2]

The verse reflects the attitude and environment of the "proper" nineteenth-century young woman. While she focused privately on her world as expressed through her pen and needle, the public image of her was being defined by the sermons, etiquette books, and literature being published on the East Coast.

Nineteenth-century women compiled a private history recorded in Bibles, diaries, letters, and needlework rather than in public documents of military, court, legislative, and town records. Much can be learned by review of the diaries and letters of the women, as well as their families and friends, who made the quilts found in today's Oregon.

The extent and role of education in their lives were as varied as their life experiences. While some learned to read and write, all learned needlework skills because of the need to make the clothes they wore and the household linens they used.

The Quilts

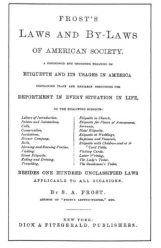

Title page of etiquette
book

Bed quilts were a major part of the household linen production in nineteenth-century America. Answering the demand for such large numbers of items, women became extremely proficient in their needlework capabilities and their work was encouraged and recognized. Many women began to spend leisure time planning and creating quilts to honor and commemorate important events in their lives. Citing an 1883 issue of *Arthur's Magazine,* which estimated as many as three quarters of the bed coverings were quilts, Elaine Hedges stated that sufficient numbers were made to allow women to create special ones meant to be kept as records of life's passages.[3]

Based on the vast extent of work in quilt history in the last twenty years, it has been accepted that quilts were the most universal form of needlework produced by all women. They were made by all socioeconomic levels of society, all ethnic groups, all cultural groups in all parts of the country. They are one of the most valid kinds of artifacts for studying the broadest range of women and their experiences throughout American history.

The Frontier Experience

In general, women's actual frontier experience was molded by several factors. Uppermost was the "shaping power" of the West as defined by historian Anne Hyde. The territory's landscapes presented new perceptual challenges forcing people to create new expressions. Studying the history of perception involves considerations of what women expected to see, what they saw, how they interpreted it, and what was learned from it. Citing not only a woman's background of experience in age and role, Hyde also noted the importance of the mode of transportation and the medium through which the perceptions were interpreted.[4]

Another factor on the frontier that shaped women's response in quilts was the sharing of resources and creative skills before, during, and after the Trail journey. Discussing particularly the experience on the Trail, Julie Roy Jeffrey quotes the following:

> There was "commendable reciprocity in the exhibition and distribution of new patchwork quilt designs. The display was made with quite as much pride as is the showing of artistic fancy-work today. All plans, patterns, ideas, or innovations were pleasantly passed along. . . . This was true, likewise, of clothing cutting. Exclusiveness in the cut or trim of apparel was unthought of."[5]

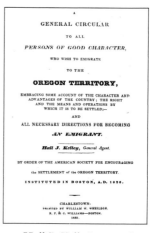

Hall J. Kelley's general circular, 1831

For women experienced in needlework, the interpretation of the Oregon Trail through their quilts was a natural creative enterprise. Themes that reflected their perceptions of the leave-taking from family and friends, the six months of living outdoors, and the reliance on equipment and divine guidance appeared in quilts connected to migration. Women translated the geometric shapes of colored fabrics into what they saw in flora and fauna and in what they experienced in weather and exposure on the Trail. They pieced, appliquéd, and quilted their response to the people and places in their new home in the West.

PART ONE
1840 – 1850

W.H. JACKSON
1937.

1843–1850

TRAIL

Primitive, isolated, no printed guides, few experienced leaders, few services available, hazardous river crossings.

Length of travel time usually seven to eight months, starting April and lasting until December.

Numbers of people going fairly small, plenty of food and water, Indians relatively peaceful.

People were upwardly mobile looking for free land and coming from free land.

QUILTS

Of the project's twenty:
Seven were quilted when came.
Nine were quilted after.
Two pieced while on trail.
Two not quilted.
One tied.

Span of time represented by quilts circa 1825–1898.

Number by year (family):
1843: 1 (1) 1847–3 (3)
1844: 2 (2) 1848–0
1845: 1 (1) 1849–2 (1)
1846: 7 (1) 1850–4 (4)

Categories of quilts:
Whole cloth: One
Appliquéd: Six
Pieced: Thirteen

Themes:
Celebration: Six
Migration: Eight
Unknown: Five

QUILT MAKERS

Age range from 14 to 51 with two unknown.
Five came with extended families.
Three with husbands.
Two with parents.
One with brother and sister.
Four making second migration.
Three making first migration.
One making third migration.

One woman died on the Trail.

Reasons for coming:
Nine came for economic and business opportunities.
Two came for land.
One against slavery.

Number of husbands who went to gold fields:
One went before bringing family.
Two went after.

Thirteen settled in the northern Willamette Valley:
Four in Marion County
Three in Yamhill County
Two in Benton and Washington Counties
One each in Clackamas and Polk

Moved again after arriving in Oregon:
Two to Douglas County in southern Oregon
One to Lake County in southeastern Oregon
One to Lane County in southern Willamette Valley

Role achieved in Oregon:
Eleven worked to establish farm and family.
One founded a church.
One used her needle skills to establish a business.

QUILTING ACTIVITY

Before:
Four quilted between zero and five years before going on Trail.
One quilted between five and fifteen and one between fifteen and twenty-five years.

After:
None quilted after getting here between zero and five years.
Four quilted between five and fifteen years.
No one between twenty-five and thirty-five years.
Two quilted after more than thirty-five years.
Elizabeth Currier Foster made one after being in Oregon sixty-four years and another after sixty-nine years.
Frances Tandy Harlow quilted one after being here forty-eight years.

The Trail Preparation

THE WEEKS, MONTHS, OR YEARS BEFORE THE planned departure were active and busy with preparation. While men dealt with the disposal of land at home and gathered the necessary supplies and livestock, women prepared the food and sewed clothes, tents, wagon covers, and bedding. Making quilts as bedding to use or to keep as heirlooms was an activity often noted in the writings of the period.

The cost estimated by the guidebooks for a family of four to move West was about six hundred dollars overland, while a voyage by ship around the Horn was six hundred dollars per person. With the exception of the very early years of migration, there were guidebooks, letters, and journals that told the preparations to make, the supplies to bring, and the routes to take including the best locations for food and water.

An interesting footnote to the list of recommended items says, "Do not leave home, or St. Louis without possessing the above Guide, also the *best map* of California etc that can be procured." The admonition sounds not unlike today's credit card commercial, "Don't leave home without it."

The recommendation for bedding was forty-five pounds at a cost of $22.50 for a party of three persons for one year when traveling with oxen. Children were to be counted as adults with no adjustment made for them.[1] Other guidebooks were more specific and suggested two or three blankets and comforters for each traveler.[2] The idea was to have sufficient bedding to last the trip and for several years after arrival in Oregon.

Quiltmaking became an important part of preparation for moving West or leaving the States as women focused on the need for bedding or retaining emotional connection with family and friends. As they made the quilts to be used on the Trail, they referred to them in diaries, letters, and logs. They made quilts to honor their families and friends who stayed behind, and they made quilts to record the items from their past. For instance, Elizabeth Currier Foster made the Poke Stalk (Quilt A–3) before emigrating with her older brother and sister to Oregon in 1846. The poke stalk plant does not exist in the Northwest.

Part of preparing for the trip meant talking to other family members to encourage them to join the migration. Persuasive

ESTIMATE OF AN OUTFIT

The following estimate of an outfit, for one year, for three persons, with ox teams, is copied from *The Emigrants' Guide to California* by Joseph E. Ware:

Four yoke of Oxen*		
$50 each		$200.00
One wagon, cover, etc.		100.00
Three rifles, $20		60.00
Three pair pistols, $15		45.00
Five barrels flour,	1,030 lbs.	20.00
Bacon,	600 "	30.00
Coffee,	100 "	8.00
Tea,	5 "	2.75
Sugar,	150 "	7.00
Rice,	75 "	3.75
Fruit, dried,	50 "	3.00
Salt, pepper, & c.,	50 "	3.00
Saleratus,	10 "	1.00
Lead,	30 "	1.20
Powder,	25 "	5.50
Tools, & c.,	25 "	7.30
Mining tools,	30 "	12.00
Tent,	30 "	5.00
Bedding,	45 "	22.50
Cooking Utensils,	30 "	4.00
Lard,	50 "	2.50
Private baggage,	150 "	
Matches,		1.00
One mule,		50.00
Candles and soap,		5.50
Total:	2,585 lbs.	$600.00

*The teams for the journey should be oxen or mules, either of which can be purchased at the frontier towns. Cows are often taken along for their milk, being sometimes the only dependable source for drink.

WESTWARD MIGRATION*

Year	Estimate
1841	100
1842	200
1843	1,000
1844	2,000
1845	5,000
1846	1,000
1847	2,000
1848	4,000
1849	30,000
1850	55,000
1851	10,000
1852	50,000
1853	20,000
1854	10,000
1855	5,000
1856	5,000
1857	5,000
1858	10,000
1859	30,000
1860	15,000
1861	5,000
1862	5,000
1863	10,000
1864	20,000
1865	25,000
1866	25,000
Total	350,000

*From *The Great Platte River Road* by Merrill Mattes.

letters were written, and visits were made among relatives. Since the family was the social unit on the Trail, often the woman's goal was to maintain that unit at all costs. Even single men and women attached themselves to family units and hired on to do specific tasks in order to travel in safer numbers. Whenever possible, families traveled with a group of friends and relatives. They would gather extended families from various places and travel West together, as did the Jacob Robbins family from Indiana (Quilt B–11).

Of special interest were the three widowed women who either came with or joined their sons and daughters. The commitment to make the long journey as an older woman shows the strength of their bond to families, although the journey might have been easier than facing loneliness without them. Mary Whitley Gilmour (Quilt B–18) knew that when she decided to travel with her daughter and family in 1852; Nancy Callaway Nye (Quilt C–6), a pioneer of 1865, realized it after seeing most of her children leave home for the West between 1847 and 1862. It is an indication of commitment the pioneers had to their families and of the need for families to look after their elders. For Sarah Moody Fuson (Quilt C–4), going to Oregon meant not going to the poor house in Missouri.

Who they came with:	1840–50	1851–55	1856–70
Parents	3	5	3
Husband	3	12	4
Extended family	5	3	1
Brother/Sister	1	0	0
Widows/adult children	0	1	2

The Trail

During the first days on the Trail, when the settlers crossed the Missouri River and headed over the plains along the Great Platte River Road, women's feelings tended to be a mixture of concern and confidence.

Popular imagery of the period referred to this section as "the Elephant" on the Great Platte River Road. Embarking on this journey in slow-moving wagon trains, the people traveled at great personal risk into a world of unknown experiences and challenges. One diarist wrote of it on the first day out, "All hands early up anxious to see the path that leads to the Elephant."[3]

Yet as long as they were healthy, eager, and confident, the women were ready to share the journey with family and friends, old and new. Life along the Trail at first tended to be relaxed and enjoyed. Although they were busy with the tasks of providing child care and preparing meals, women still found time to appreciate each other and their surroundings. Often they would walk or ride and chat together. Catherine Haun wrote in 1849:

Seeing the Elephant

> During the day, we womenfolk visited from wagon to wagon or congenial friends spent an hour walking, ever westward, and talking over our home life back in "the states"; telling of the loved ones left behind; voicing our hopes for the future . . . and even whispering a little friendly gossip of emigrant life.[4]

Women continued their normal routine tasks of baking, washing, mending, sewing, and child care. Doing these tasks kept women focused on their domestic roles. It gave them some assurance of control over the adverse physical environment, and the repetition of this routine provided a sense of importance. As Charlotte Stearns Pengra noted in her 1853 diary on May 18:

> . . . washed a very large washing, unpacked dried and packed clothing—made a pair of calico cases for pillows and cooked two meals—done brave, I think. Those who come this journey should have their pillows covered with dark calico and sheets colored, white is not suitable.[5]

Women went prepared to do their needlework, as demonstrated by several of the important artifacts given to public collections. A gourd used to hold the yarn as a woman knit is a treasure in the Douglas County Museum of History and Natural History in Roseburg, Oregon. A pair of scissors kicked up from the dust at a burial site is another treasure, housed in the Lane County Museum of History in Eugene, Oregon. Several needlework items remain from the family of Sanford and Maria Watson, pioneers of 1849. A "housewife," the holder for personal items and needlework tools once sewn to the lining of a wagon, is now at the DAR Pioneer Mothers Cabin at Champoeg State Park. A needlebook, made by Selina Venable of Springfield, Illinois, as a gift for Virginia Watson, was given to the Oregon Historical Society by her great-granddaughter Virginia Ann Woodworth in 1935.

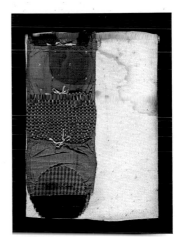

Housewife brought by Watson family

For some women, this was one of the first times they had been confronted with being on their own and totally responsible for the homelike setting. These were the newlyweds and the women who had previously had slaves to assist in their work.

Teenage Rachel Bond, pioneer of 1853, works long and hard at the cooking and clean-up. Her young husband, Allen, toils into the night tending the herd and keeping the wagons tarred and greased. The two young people got married and joined Uncle Vincent's (McClure) train without money or rigs and supplies of their own— so they've agreed to work their way to Oregon.

Rachel has found an old discarded copper kettle along the road-side, not too bruised she thinks. And as she walks westward she runs a needle and thread through squares of old fabric, storing each stitched piece inside the kettle hanging from her arm like a hand-bag. She tells Allen she'll have enough of these pieces sewn by the end of the trip to make a quilt. He agrees. That's about all they will have—a kettle and a quilt—but it's worth it.[6]

Sharing of Tasks on Trail

As wagon trains moved westward, with parties splitting up and situations changing, women on the Trail showed their commitment to the trip by being willing to perform the additional chores usually regarded as a male's. These included such tasks as pitching tents, gathering wood and buffalo chips for fires, loading and unloading wagons, yoking oxen, and driving teams. On the other hand, men also did women's work, especially if they were single or if their wives were ill. "A man assuming female responsibilities was doing a favor. A woman doing a male job was doing what was necessary."[7]

Women were also interested in the economies of the trip—the mileage covered, the quality of water and grasses, the cost of supplies. They carefully noted these figures in their diaries along with notes about grave sites, Indian encounters, births, and deaths.

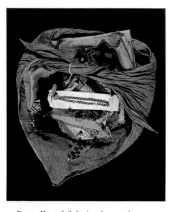

Bundle of fabrics brought on trail by Rachel Bond

Layover Days

Most trains had a "laid over" day at regular intervals to wash and do other chores not possible to be accomplished during the regular "nooning" or in the evening at camp. Washdays occurred about every two weeks when the whole train would participate in doing their laundry. Layover days were also used to clean and air the wagons, dry the bedding and clothing after one of the frequent heavy rains, and to repack the load.

Interior of covered wagon

Size of Trains

The 1846 wagon train that brought fourteen-year-old Elizabeth Currier Foster and her brother and sister to Oregon was called the Applegate Southern Cutoff Train. There were fifty wagons at the start, but after they got past the worst danger from Indian attack, they divided because there were too many cattle to manage.

Most trains would have about twelve wagons, with each driver having his turn at the head of the line. They rotated positions each day so that everyone would take their turns at the end in the dust.

By comparison, the 1863 wagon train from Bethel, Missouri, to Aurora, Oregon, was made up of forty-two wagons and 252 people making up fourteen companies.

A feature of the wagons used by William and Margaret Fuson Lieuallen (Quilt C–3, 4) was that they were built with two floors. The space between the floors stored imperishable foods such as wheat, corn, and garden seeds. If there was a death in a caravan, each wagon would contribute a board from the false floor to build the coffin.[8]

A–1

Quilt: TUFTED WHITE ON WHITE

Category: Whole cloth

Size: 86" x 73½"

Date: circa 1825

Maker: Mary ("Polly") Green Scoggin Chambers (1809–1890)

Year Over Trail: 1845

Came: As a wife with second husband, James Washington Chambers; five children; his parents, Thomas and Latitia Delzel Chambers, and six children; and his brother and wife, David and Elizabeth Chambers

County Where Settled: Washington County, Oregon

Full view of White on White quilt

The earliest quilt found that connected to the Oregon Trail was this white-on-white quilt, a rare find today, especially in the Northwest. These were made during the first decades of the nineteenth century in the East. From the published sources available, they are found in the major East Coast collections. One in the Metropolitan Museum is similar to a number of whitework pieces with drawnwork panels that were made in Kentucky.[9]

This quilt has several unusual features. It is made of a whole cloth with no seam lines. Fine white fabric of this quality was available in a wide width.[10] The featured technique is tufted candlewicking, using a thick thread. One aid in dating this quilt is that thread-intensive quilting was dependent upon an inexpensive and plentiful supply of cotton thread that became available around 1810.[11]

The classic design is a central medallion of leaves and flowers with a center bloom and four radiating blooms and leaves into each quadrant. This is surrounded by a vine of grape clusters and leaves. Then, toward the edge, centered on each of the four sides, is a star. The stars on the sides and top match with a small circle in the center. The star at the top has a bird beside it. The fourth star, on the bottom, is composed of diamond segments. These motifs are similar in style and format to those used on bed rugs in the seventeenth and eighteenth centuries in Europe and America. The major difference is that the bed rugs are a form of needlepoint with the surface entirely covered by rich textile stitches, while the quilt has just the outline of the design in running stitch that is tufted. The simple explanation is that the need for a heavy bed rug was not felt in the warmer climate of Kentucky as it was in New England.[12]

The quilting design is an outline, or echo, where one to three lines of stitching surround each of the motifs. There is also a gridwork of diamonds filling in various open spaces of the quilt.

A marking of initials, or extra motif that was stitched with quilting thread in the lower center front, may be an identification clue. Because of the age and use of the quilt, it is hard to interpret.

Detail of bird and star

Machine-stitched lines along the edges of the quilt were added later as a means of stabilization. The replacement binding is a commercially made tape.

The quilt's maker, Mary Green, was born in 1809 to the Reverend John and Rachel Mackey Green in Kentucky. She was married in 1828 to Woodson Scoggin; her sister Sarah married Woodson's brother James. Both were sons of John Scoggin of White County, Tennessee. Woodson and Mary Scoggin settled in either Cooper or Morgan County, Missouri, in the early 1830s.[13]

Woodson died on January 25, 1840, leaving Mary with five children under the age of eleven. She married Dr. James Washington Chambers in 1844. They came West in 1845 with his extended family, arriving in December two weeks before their first child was born. According to the *Oregon Territory 1850 Census,* they were living with her five children, their two children, and five other unrelated men between the ages of eighteen and forty-five in Washington County, Oregon.[14]

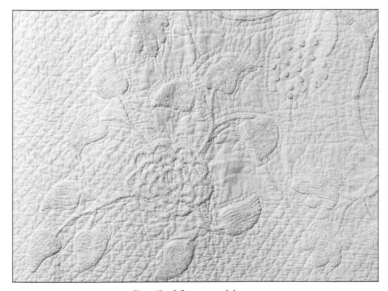

Detail of flower and leaves

A museum donation record states the quilt was given to Martha P. I. Scoggin for a wedding present when she married C. B. Comstock in 1853. The quilt was given to the Lane County Museum in Eugene, Oregon, by LaVella Young Gilbert, granddaughter of Mr. and Mrs. Comstock.[15]

A–2

Quilt: RED AND GREEN TULIP

Category: Appliqué

Size: 82″ x 70″

Date: circa 1840

Maker: Sally Hull Perkins (1789–1876)

Year Over Trail: 1844

Came: As a wife with husband, Eli, four married children and their families, and one unmarried son, Joel

County Where Settled: Yamhill County, Oregon

Full view of Red and Green Tulip

The simple appliqué tulip pattern was common in the mid-nineteenth century. The orange fabric was produced commercially by the 1840s with mineral dyes.[16] The quilting pattern of lines grouped in threes uses the format known as fan or elbow quilting. According to Sally's great-granddaughter Iona Westerfield, who gave the quilt to the Yamhill County Museum, Sally made the quilt before she came to Oregon and brought it with her in 1844.

Sally Hull Perkins was born October 3, 1789, in Vermont. According to family history, her father, Matthew Hull, was kidnapped by British sailors off a beach in Dublin, Ireland, and, with a school friend, was brought to America where he was compelled to fight for the British. Sally married Eli Perkins on March 6, 1809 at Warsaw, Genessee County, New York. They had seven children born between 1811 and 1828.

In 1832 they moved to Tippecanoe County, Indiana.

The Perkins family were part of the 1,400 people who made the trek in 1844. Coming at this time, they found a lack of housing and few

people in Oregon. The winter of 1844–45 is recorded as being particularly difficult in Oregon.[17] With two business partners, Eli Perkins built the first sawmills and gristmill in Yamhill County. In 1846–47, their son Joel founded the town of Lafayette, the first town on the western side of the Willamette River above the falls at Oregon City.

Sally Hull Perkins

ELIZABETH FOSTER

The next six quilts, made by Elizabeth Currier Foster over a span of almost seventy years, offer a unique and complete history of one woman's Trail experience as expressed in her needlework. Her life and work have been meticulously recorded by her daughter, Lulu Foster Schminck, and lovingly treasured at the Schminck Memorial Museum in Lakeview, Oregon. Covering a significant span of time and place in Oregon, these completed quilts represent the joy and satisfaction quiltmaking brought to one specific woman, a pioneer of 1846.

After a study of the collection, it appears that Elizabeth brought this legacy of quilts and quilting in her trunk to Oregon in 1846. The first Poke Stalk (Quilt A–3) and a fragment of Star (Quilt A–4) were brought as completed quilts. The next two, Flying Star (Quilt A–4) and a Rose of Sharon (Quilt A–5), were brought as partially completed projects. A set of fabric templates for a Mexican Lily (Quilt A–6) and additional fabrics that would appear in other quilts were packed away.

The early family history reveals a tragic life for a young girl. Elizabeth Currier Foster was born on June 18, 1832, in Irisburg, Orleans County, Vermont. Soon thereafter, the family moved to Massachusetts and New York. In 1844 they settled in Andrew County, Missouri, where her mother, Elizabeth Smith Currier, died suddenly of a flulike ailment. One year later, in 1845, her father, Jacob Currier, died of a broken heart.

In 1846 three young Currier adults—Sarah Currier Humphrey, age twenty-four; Jacob Manley Currier, age nineteen; and Elizabeth B. Currier, age fourteen—along with Sarah's husband, A. L. Humphrey—started for Oregon. Traveling via wagon and ox team, they crossed the Missouri River on May 10, 1846. The record of Elizabeth's Trail experience is fairly complete through her reminiscences and mementoes as well as journals of others on the trip. She had time to enjoy her friends and to appreciate the places she saw. She did her westering tasks with her family members, including herding cattle by riding horseback.

For the last part of their journey, they were members of the first wagon train Jesse Applegate led over the proposed southern cut-off across the Black Rock Desert of Nevada and the Goose Lake Valley in northern California. The trail, which became known as the Applegate Trail, turned south and west at Fort Hall and came into the southern end of the Willamette Valley, thereby avoiding the dangerous raft and canoe trips down the Columbia River and mountain crossings of the Blues and Cascades.

During this phase, an accident happened that made a lasting impression upon her and, later, her own family. The younger sister of her friend Lucy Henderson Deady died after an overdose of medicine. Elizabeth was so saddened that she cut a beaded flower from her bag and laid it on the grave.*

She noted waiting sixteen days for the Applegate Trail to be cut out in the Calpooia Mountains of southern Oregon. She and her sister were the first women to go through the Cow Creek Canyon, not an easy task for anyone. They finally arrived December 5, 1846, in Polk County where they spent the winter sheltered by a family in Rickreall.

Later she moved to the Philomath area in neighboring Benton County, where she married James Foster in

Elizabeth Currier Foster, circa 1850

1848 at age sixteen. A year later her sister, Sarah Currier Humphrey, died. In 1850 her brother, Jacob Manley Currier, married Maria Foster, Elizabeth's sister-in-law.

At this time as a young wife and mother, she returned to making quilts. The Double Irish Chain I (Quilt A–5) was completed in 1852. In 1854 she completed the Rose of Sharon and started work on the Mexican Lily, only to be interrupted by family needs.

By 1869 she had given birth to eleven babies. The three surviving girls are in the accompanying photo with the Newhouse sisters, their neighbors. Four sons had survived, although one died at age twelve in August 1869. A twelfth baby, Luvia, was born in November 1869.

In 1873 the Foster family of ten moved to southeastern Oregon to a drier, healthier climate. Here, on Summer Lake in Lake County, they built a ranch, later known for its fine produce, cattle, and racehorses. Their ranch was one of the most magnificent in the valley, producing nearly every variety of fruit. The house, built with space for a ballroom that could be curtained off for dormitory sleeping, became the center for hospitality in the region.

Here Elizabeth's last two children, Ralph and Lulu, were born and raised. Lulu is the daughter who started the family museum with her husband in the 1930s.

Continuing to live on the ranch after her husband's death in 1909, Elizabeth returned to quilting. The Double Irish Chain (Quilt A–9) was made in 1912, and the Mexican Lily, started in 1854, was completed in 1915.

Elizabeth also traveled to visit ten surviving children and shared her past with friends, family, and at pioneer reunions. A 1913 newspaper clipping from the Schminck scrapbook describes a trip she took alone at age eighty-one from her home in southeastern Oregon to Portland to attend a reunion and visit family. It reads in part:

Notwithstanding her advanced age, Mrs. Foster enjoys traveling and is perfectly able to take care of herself among strangers. She is a great reader and is more familiar with national politics than many of the

Elizabeth Currier Foster and her young daughters with Newhouse sisters, circa 1869

younger generations, and discusses modern events with the same intelligence and enjoyment as she does those happenings of the earlier history of Oregon.[18]

These quilts are part of the extensive collection at the Schminck Memorial Museum in Lakeview, Oregon. The museum houses the well-documented family history, scrapbooks, and extensive collections of more than 5,000 pieces representing the life span of two Oregon families. It was a life's project of the Fosters' youngest daughter, Lulu Foster Schminck, and her husband, Dalpheus, a retail clerk in the local general store for more than fifty years. The museum is administered by the Oregon State Society of the Daughters of the American Revolution.

Home of James and Elizabeth Foster, circa 1855

*An account of the accidental death of Salita Jane Henderson is explained on page 43.

A–3

Quilt: POKE STALK

Category: Appliqué

Size: 82" x 76"

Date: 1845

Maker: Elizabeth Currier Foster
(1832–1921)

Year Over Trail: 1846

Came: As an orphan with brother
Jacob Manley Currier and sister
Sarah Currier Humphrey and
Sarah's husband

County Where Settled: Polk County,
Benton County, then Lake
County, Oregon

Full view of Poke Stalk

The first quilt, Poke Stalk, is a
unique design, which indicates a
sense of migration. More commonly
known as poke weed or pokeberry
(Phytolacca decandra or *Phytolacca
americana),* the plant was a tall herb
native to the eastern part of North
America but not grown in the West.
It was used in the early homes for
many purposes. The reddish purple
berries and purple root were used in
medicine. The young green leaves
and shoots were edible and used in
salads. The roots and berries provided a weak dye that tended to
stain rather than dye. The red color
also faded toward brown.[19]

The reason Elizabeth chose this
plant for her quilt design is not
recorded, but speculation would indicate that it had special meaning for
her and was something she wished
to record with her needle. Her work
is realistic including the use of pink
for the stems.

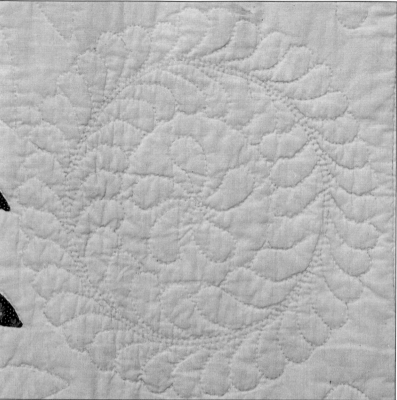

Detail of wreath

The quilt reveals personality traits she is known to have exhibited: a sense of self-discipline and determination combined with a joyous whimsy. There are 554 small, raised red berries. The appliquéd vases laid on the intersections of blocks show a whimsical sense in the placement of the stems. The quilting patterns include outline quilting around the appliqué work and a repeat of the appliquéd leaf radiating from the stems or scattered over the quilt's surface. There are also six traditional ten-inch wreaths quilted at regular intervals not far from the vine border. The workmanship in the quilting varies.

She was thirteen in 1845 when the quilt was made, which leads to the speculation it may have been completed by family and friends in celebration of her work or in preparation for leave-taking.

Detail of vase

Detail of stalk

A–4

Quilt: STAR

Category: Pieced

Size: 86½" x 67", a fragment

Date: circa 1840

Maker: Member of the Currier family

Year Over Trail: 1846

Brought: With Elizabeth Currier Foster and her brother and sister

County Where Settled: Polk County, Benton County, then Lake County, Oregon

This fragment is included because it represents the interest of Elizabeth Currier Foster and her daughter to retain a quilt treasure, in spite of its tattered condition. It had long been a noninventoried item until the connection was made to another quilt in the collection.

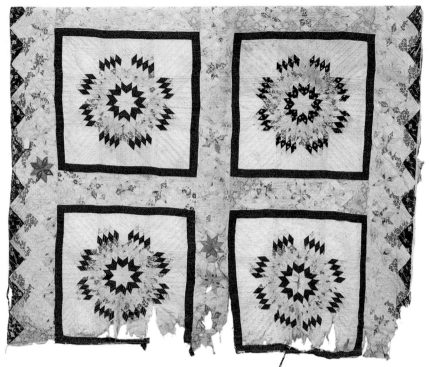

Full view of Star

Detail of wreath

The vivid indigo-blue triangles along the edge are the same fabric as that of the Double Irish Chain made in 1852.

The fabrics are those of the early nineteenth-century textile production. The six large stars and the smaller four-inch stars are composed of diamond-shaped pieces.

A–5

Quilt: DOUBLE IRISH CHAIN I

Category: Pieced

Size: 80″ x 68″

Date: 1852

Maker: Elizabeth Currier Foster
   (1832–1921)

Year Over Trail: 1846

Came: As a very young woman with
   brother and sister

County Where Settled: Polk County,
   Benton County, then Lake
   County, Oregon

The indigo-blue and white fabric of this quilt was brought across the plains with the Curriers. It is present in the pieced Star fragment shown in Quilt A–4.

The Double Irish Chain pattern can be interpreted as a migration pattern when the design element of line is considered. The line defines and connects two points and creates a sense of visual movement. Looking at the Double Irish Chain quilt, the eye is carried across the surface by the diagonal line formed by color and placement of the squares.

Detail of quilting

Detail of fabric

Full view of Double Irish Chain I

A–6

Quilt: ROSE OF SHARON

Category: Appliqué

Size: 90″ x 80″

Date: 1854

Maker: Elizabeth Currier Foster
(1832–1921)

Year Over Trail: 1846

Came: As a very young woman with
brother and sister

County Where Settled: Polk County,
Benton County, then Lake
County, Oregon

Block with eight blossoms,
five fully developed and
three less defined

This fourth quilt, Rose of Sharon,
continues the illustration of quilts as
a representation of a woman's migration experience.

From examination, it would seem
that the blocks were started "while
in the States," packed away, and
brought out to complete in 1854
after the quiltmaker had been in
Oregon for eight years. The reasons
for this supposition are as follows:

The large roses in the nine blocks
have the same fabrics as the 1845
Poke Stalk quilt, indicating the fabric
was probably acquired at the same
time and place. Supplies and stores
were not prevalent in the 1840s.

Of the nine blocks, four were
completed with the *same* four fabrics
throughout. These four have eight
floral blossoms with seven fully
shaped petals each.

A fifth block almost matches except for four leaves done in a second
green print, and the centers of three
of the eight blossoms are of a different pink print. It also has a mixture
of the five fully sculpted blossoms
and three more rounded blooms.
This may indicate it was almost
completed before the quiltmaker ran
short of fabrics and had to change
the style of the bloom. The fully
developed blooms would be more
difficult and would take more time
to complete.

Block with two patterns of green
cloth

Block with one pieced and appliquéd
flower

The remaining four blocks have a
significant amount of the second
green fabric appearing in the stems
and leaves of each of the blocks.
With two exceptions, they have buds
instead of blooms at the ends of the
stems. One block has a single pieced
and appliquéd flower. The other
block has seven appliquéd stems and
buds, with the eighth being quilted.

The placement of the quilting designs reveals much the same format
as the Poke Stalk quilt. Outline, or
echo, quilting is combined with additional leaves along the stems; and
designs of circles, crescents, and

flowers are scattered whimsically
over the surface.

The border and the binding are
machine-stitched while the blocks
are joined by hand. Elizabeth Currier Foster's small sewing machine at
the museum has the earliest patent
date of March 7, 1854, and the last
of November 18, 1867, indicating it
was purchased after the 1867 date.
The possibility exists that a sewing
machine came into her home at an
earlier date, since machines were extremely popular and available in the
Willamette Valley area where she was
living.

Full view of Rose of Sharon

Detail of center blocks of early fabrics

A–7

Quilt: FLYING STAR

Category: Pieced

Size: 82" x 72"

Date: 1844 Started
        1910 Finished

Maker: Elizabeth Currier Foster
(1832–1921)

Year Over Trail: 1846

Came: As a very young woman,
with her brother and sister

County Where Settled: Polk County,
Benton County, then Lake
County, Oregon

The Flying Star illustrates the major focus and activity of the mid-nineteenth century, that of migration. The pattern, along with its name from the museum records, is similar to others, such as Kansas Troubles, Grandmother's Pinwheel, and Delectable Mountains, which give the same sense of movement when the blocks are grouped by color in units of four.

In studying the quilt and reading from the left, one sees fourteen rows of five-and-one-fourth-inch blocks. Rows six, seven, and eight were begun in 1844 before the young people came West. The fabrics represented here are a rainbow print of shades from blue to green of roller-printed fabrics. The white fabric in these three rows is of a different grade and shade than in the other rows. The outer rows represent Elizabeth's return to the project in the early 1900s. The prints are from the period between 1890 and 1910, including the black-and-white mourning prints, the gray-blues, the black prints with bright colors, and the number of pinks.[20] The blocks are set together with machine stitching rather than hand stitching. The elbow, or fan, quilting has a radius of ten inches with ten lines spaced an inch apart. Some of the lines have the same blue marking as the Rose of Sharon quilt.

Detail of edge and four-square blocks

Full view of Flying Star

A–8

Quilt: DOUBLE IRISH CHAIN II

Category: Pieced

Size: 90" x 78"

Date: 1912

Maker: Elizabeth Currier Foster (1832–1921)

Year Over Trail: 1846

Came: As a very young woman with brother and sister

County Where Settled: Polk County, Benton County, then Lake County, Oregon

This quilt shows the continuing tradition of Elizabeth's work with the patterns and fabrics she had already used in earlier quilts. The Double Irish Chain pattern is the same as the one she made dated 1852. The pink fabric is the same as used in the Rose of Sharon, dated 1854. The mitered-corner border treatment is new with this quilt and would be repeated in the 1915 Mexican Lily.

At this time in her life, in 1909, her husband of sixty-one years had died at their Summer Lake ranch home in Lake County in southeastern Oregon.

Full view of Double Irish Chain II

Detail showing pink fabrics

A–9

Quilt: MEXICAN LILY

Category: Appliqué

Size: 86″ x 84″

Date: 1854 Started
1915 Finished

Maker: Elizabeth Currier Foster
(1832–1921)

Year Over Trail: 1846

Came: As a very young woman with
brother and sister

County Where Settled: Polk County,
Benton County, then Lake
County, Oregon

Full view of Mexican Lily

Examination of the appliquéd vase and flowers reveals two clues that connect this quilt to the period before the migration and leads to the conclusion that the templates for the pattern were cut and brought over the Trail. There is one pattern piece for each element of the design in the same green and red fabrics as the Poke Stalk quilt. However, the fact that these pattern pieces are not on the same block leads to the conclusion that a block was not constructed, but instead the individual pieces were cut and used for a pattern when the additional pieces were cut and assembled at the time recorded by the family, 1854. In the process of cutting and stacking the pieces for the appliqué work, the two fabrics were mixed in and ended up on different blocks. The appliqué work also shows a whimsy in the shaping of the stems and flowers that adds personality but also, perhaps, reveals less attention to detail by Elizabeth, now a wife and mother of two young boys.

Sarah Currier Humphrey's death in 1849 may also have a bearing on this quilt. If the pieces were cut as a pattern design reference when the women lived in Missouri, perhaps before their mother died, Sarah may have helped to appliqué the pattern.

Comparison of fabric placement and evidence of whimsy

By 1854 Sarah was gone, and Elizabeth was left to do the work and set the blocks together.

A finish date of 1915 is reflected by the mitered corners of the single border. The primary quilting design is an outline of the appliqué work with the secondary pattern being a grid of lines drawn in pencil. Both features would have taken considerable time to complete.

A–10

Quilt: LILY

Category: Appliqué

Size: 81" x 73"

Date: circa 1850

Maker: Sarah Hammond Buell (1800–1885)

Year Over Trail: 1847

Came: As a wife with husband, Elias, and seven children

County Where Settled: Polk County, Oregon

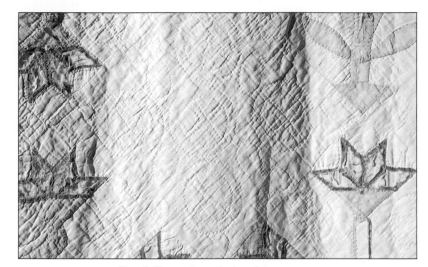

Detail illustrating wheel quilting pattern

This quilt of solid red and green prints in a pieced and appliquéd lily pattern offers early evidence of a migration motif. The wheel design quilted in the solid white blocks is represented by four circles surrounding a center circle with double lines bisecting the centers of each. Also in the blocks are little hearts quilted in each corner. Knowing that hearts have long been used to connote sentiments of love in wedding quilts and other needlework, it is believed the wheel represents divine guidance during "leave-taking" or migration.

The quilt is carefully made with attention to detail. Each of the stems is folded to fit the space of the block and to shape the design. There are three narrow borders of each of the quilt's colors on two sides and a wide green border on the other two sides.

Family history indicates the quilt was made by Sarah as she journeyed across the plains. This may be true, but a comparison with quilts of the period suggests the careful piecing and appliqué work would have been hard to plan and place while moving or in the temporary location of a camp. The number and size of borders indicate that she had time to handpiece each of them in place. The amount of quilting in each block is more like that of quilts completed in the East before coming West. The quilt probably was completed before the trip and brought with the family.

Sarah Hammond Buell was born January 22, 1800, in Liberty, Frederick County, Maryland, and died in Sheridan, Polk County, Oregon, in 1885. She married Elias Buell on October 19, 1817, in Allensville, Switzerland County, Indiana. They arrived in Oregon in 1847, and by 1855 he had built the first sawmills and gristmill on Mill Creek near Buell, Oregon.[21]

According to family history, the quilt was a wedding gift to their daughter Melissa. She met her future husband, Isaac Hinshaw, on the wagon train en route to Oregon. He and his nine-year-old son, Sanford, were coming to Oregon for a new start after the death of his wife. Melissa Buell and Isaac Hinshaw were married in Gooseneck Valley, Polk County, Oregon. They eventually had eight children.

The quilt remained with Melissa Buell Hinshaw throughout her life and then passed through her family to a great-granddaughter, JoAnn Wiss. In 1982, realizing the value of

Elias and Sarah Hammond Buell

the antique quilt to historians, she donated it to the Horner Museum on the campus of Oregon State University.[22]

Full view of Lily

A–11

Quilt: WHEEL OF FORTUNE

Category: Pieced

Size: 82½" x 72"

Date: 1848

Maker: Lavina Elizabeth Frazier Wright (1829–1912)

Year Over Trail: 1843

Came: As a daughter with stepfather and mother, William and Sarah Russell McHaley, and two brothers and one sister

County Where Settled: Marion County, Clackamas County, Oregon

The old Wright farmhouse, 1876

This popular nineteenth-century pattern is one with a variety of names reflecting the area or purpose for which it was made. The name Wheel of Fortune calls to mind the migration experience of Lavina Elizabeth Frazier Wright on one of the first wagon trains over the Trail in 1843. This journey, under the leadership of Jesse Applegate, was especially long and difficult since it was necessary to clear the route as the group traveled. It was particularly harrowing to be stranded on the edge of the Columbia River for four or five days with no food or shelter until the party was rescued by Dr. John McLaughlin from Fort Vancouver.

The quilt, pieced of solid colors, has several interesting features. The reds are of two different shades, indicating the maker ran short of the first fabric and carefully placed the second in the upper left and lower center so it would not detract from the visual effect of the quilt. Two colors of quilting thread are used: red and aqua. Sometimes in quilts of this era, the quilting thread will pick up the dye of the fabric and change colors; but that is not the case here where the colors are in the white areas of the quilt. The quilt has

elbow quilting in rows one inch apart and a flower quilted in the center of the white area.

Lavina Elizabeth Frazier was born March 16, 1828, in Bloomfield, Monroe County, Indiana, to Randall and Sarah Russell Frazier. Her father died in Bloomfield, and her mother then married William McHaley. The family joined the wagon train led by Jesse Applegate heading to Oregon in 1843.[23]

Lavina married Harrison Wright on February 22, 1847, settling on his donation land claim in Clackamas County near Mollala. After the birth of their first son, Harrison Wright went to the gold fields of California in 1849. He returned, not with gold but with a herd of Spanish long horn cattle which he used to start a cattle business. Over the years, Lavina and he had eleven children, the second youngest being Elizabeth Wright, born in 1865, to whom the quilt was given.

While attending the legislature in Salem in 1870, Harrison contracted

Lavina Elizabeth Frazier Wright

smallpox. Upon his return home, he exposed his family to the disease. Fortunately, a knowledgeable neighbor, Sam Oakley, knew how to culture a cowpox vaccine that countered the effects of the smallpox. In the end, the father and the youngest child, a baby, died of the disease. The others all survived.[24]

Full view of Wheel of Fortune

A–12

Quilt: PIN WHEEL

Category: Pieced

Size: 81¾" x 77½"

Date: 1849

Maker: Sarah Koontz Glover (1803–1885)

Year Over Trail: 1849

Came: As a wife with husband, Philip Glover, and eight of their children, including James Nettle Glover, who would later found Spokane, Washington; his brother John Glover; and sister-in-law Matilda Glover Koontz, wife of Nicholas Koontz who had come in 1847.

County Where Settled: Marion County, Oregon

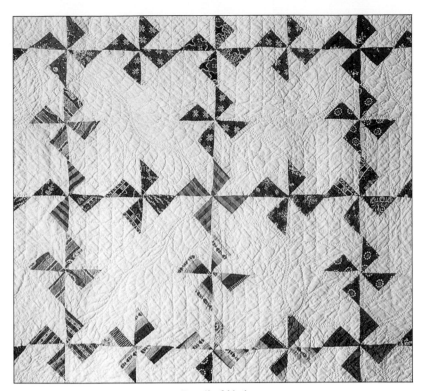

Detail of block

The hand-pieced quilt, primarily brown with some greens and blues, was hand-pieced while on the Trail. The wheel motif in the quilt's design gives a sense of movement as might be experienced in the slow-moving wagons and by the blowing wind. It is particularly effective with the blocks set "on point." The quilting further reflects the Trail and nature in the simple vinelike design of flowers and leaves.

Attached to the quilt is a penciled note by Mabel C. Glover Root, the maker's granddaughter, which says it was made "while crossing the plains in 1849."[25]

Sarah Koontz was born April 13, 1803, in Missouri, the daughter of Nicholas and Rebecca McConnell Koontz, who had migrated from Pennsylvania. She met Philip Glover, a native of Maryland, at her father's tavern on the Boonslick Trace west

of St. Charles, Missouri. The family story about the incident says she was so overcome by the appearance of the handsome, distinguished-looking Philip that she had to retire to the rear of the cabin where she sat down on a wine cask and cried. The couple were married in November 1819. They lived in a flint rock house built on the line between Lincoln and Warren counties in eastern Missouri.

Theirs was a prosperous farm with fertile fields, substantial orchards and buildings, and a "great swarm of slaves." The flint rock house had the slave quarters nearby and a large open fronting space where, family history relates, Philip Glover would walk bareheaded in the violent storms carrying his Bible. It was said

that his presence and calm, reassuring words would allay the fears of the slaves that the world was coming to an end.

This ability was again recognized when, in 1849, he was chosen leader of the train of fifty wagons to leave the racial strife of Missouri and head for Oregon.

The family traveled with three wagons, coming into the Willamette Valley by way of the Barlow Road after a journey of six months and a day. Their oldest son, William, having come in 1848, was there to meet them. The area they claimed was between the Salem prairie and the Waldo hills of Marion County.

Full view of Pin Wheel

A–13

Quilt: WHEEL PATTERN

Category: Pieced

Size: 83¾" x 71½"

Date: 1849 started
     Finished later

Maker: Sarah Koontz Glover (1803–
     1885)

Year Over Trail: 1849

Came: As a wife with husband,
     Philip Glover, and extended family

County Where Settled: Marion
     County, Oregon

This quilt was noted by the family as being pieced while crossing the plains in 1849. From study of the quilt, family history, and discussions with the current owner, it was agreed that it was finished later—perhaps after Sarah's husband died in 1872. She was known then to have spent time on her needlework while staying at her daughter's house.

The quilt's most significant fact is the identification of the pattern as being a wheel. This accords with the thesis that quilts were made to reflect the women's experience of migration. The placement of the red and green colors gives the sense of circular movement.

After Philip Glover died in 1872, Sarah Koontz Glover spent much of her time in the home of her youn-

Detail of block

gest daughter, Lou Glover Culver, west of her old homestead. She was described as neatness and dexterity personified, always making sure that things were done just right. Because her eyesight remained strong, she was able to do much needlework. "Some of the prized possessions in our family being quilts in beautiful designs which she 'pieced' and quilted. I have one in a wheel pat-tern in green, red, and white which she gave to Father."[26]

Although generally this is referred to as a star pattern, it is a widely produced pattern with at least twelve names.[27]

Full view of Wheel Pattern

A–14

Quilt: SUN PATTERN BLOCKS/
HEXAGON QUILT BLOCKS

Category: Pieced

Size: Unfinished

Date: 1850

Maker: Mary Helen Venable Medley
(1817–1851)

Year Over Trail: 1850

Came: As a wife with husband, John
Medley; their seven children; her
parents, Nathaniel and Mary Venable; their two children; her sister
and husband, Martha Frances and
Harrison Pinkston, and their family

County Where Settled: Clackamas
County, then Douglas County,
Oregon

Block of pieced Sun pattern

Hexagon blocks (below)

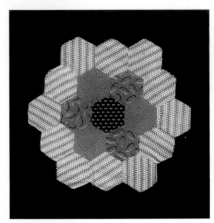

This museum gift consists of two
sets of blocks. One, a small set of a
sun pattern, may have been taken
apart from a project because there
are needle holes along the edge seam
lines. The fabrics appear to be early
nineteenth-century prints. The other,
a larger set of pieced hexagons in
various stages of completion,
represents a broader range of fabrics.
Prior to their departure from Davies
County, Missouri, John Medley had
a general store.

The acquisition document states
that these blocks were pieced by
Mary Helen Venable Medley while
crossing the plains. On the journey,
tragedy struck the family on June 11,
1850. Mary Helen's mother, Mary
Venable, and her sister, Martha
Frances Pinkston, both died,
probably of cholera. They were
buried along the Trail.

Within a year after their arrival,
Mary Helen died in Clackamas
County on July 24, 1851. John
Medley then took his family to the
Umpqua River in southern Oregon
where the other members of the
Venable family had settled. The

Hexagon blocks

brother-in-law, Harrison Pinkston,
eventually married his deceased
wife's sister, Maria Louisa Venable.

It is an appropriate tribute and
celebration of Mary Helen Venable

Medley and, possibly, her mother
and sister that the blocks were left
unfinished and given to the Douglas
County Museum of History and
Natural History.

A—15

Quilt: FLASHING MINNOW

Category: Pieced

Size: 79½" x 70"

Date: 1852

Maker: Lucinda Cox Brown Allen Spencer

Year Over Trail: 1847

Came: As a wife with husband, Elias Brown, and three children; her father, Thomas Cox; her twin sister Malinda with her husband who was a brother of Elias Brown; and other family members

County Where Settled: Marion County, then Benton County, Oregon

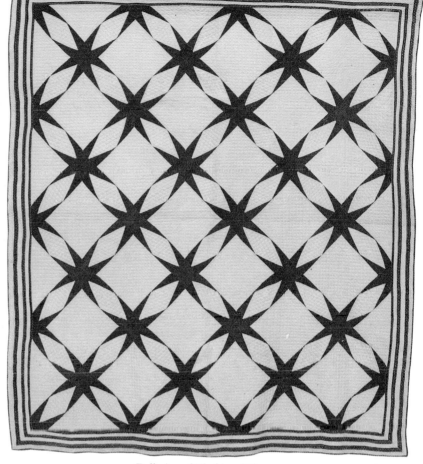

Full view of Flashing Minnow

The name of this brown and white quilt is derived from the white diamond piece darting around the brown square as a minnow flashes in water. Quilt historian Lenice Bacon referred to the pattern as "Darting Minnow."[28]

The use of just three fabrics in construction indicates there were sufficient quantities available to Lucinda Brown so that she could design the quilt using a set number of fabrics. Her father, a merchant in the Midwest, had decided to come to Oregon to establish a business to serve the many emigrants.

The quilting is extensive, with straight lines one-fourth inch apart and grid work of squares one-half inch apart.

Lucinda Cox Brown Allen Spencer was an example of the young married woman who, through her commitment to husband and family, agreed to come West, leaving behind three graves of her infants. Additional tragedy soon faced her. As a result of swimming and herding the

teams across the Platte River, Elias Brown became ill and died. He was buried in the middle of the Trail, and the wagons driven over his grave to hide it from predators.

Arriving in Oregon as part of the first wagon train to use the Barlow Road along the south side of Mount Hood, the family settled in Salem. The father built a two-story building, with the store on the lower level and living quarters above.

To support her family, Lucinda used her sewing skills to make silk hats. She also plaited wheat straw for bonnets and hats and decorated

them with ribbons. By 1849 she had established her own claim of land outside of Salem. In 1851 she married Hiram Allen whose wife had died crossing the plains, and they had four children. Living near Corvallis, then called Marysville, she helped to make two hundred pies for the first Fourth of July celebration held there. After Allen died of typhoid fever, she married George Washington Spencer whose first wife had died coming to Oregon. The last of her eight children was born in 1861.[29]

A–16

Quilt: HARLOW ALBUM QUILT

Category: Pieced

Size: 86" x 69½"

Date: 1898

Maker: Frances Burris Tandy Harlow (1815–1911)

Year Over Trail: 1850

Came: As a wife with husband, Mahlon Hall Harlow, and six children; her mother, Sarah Snelling Tandy; and possibly other family members

County Where Settled: Yamhill County, then Lane County, Oregon

Mahlon and Frances Burris Harlow and their family, circa 1890

This album quilt contains thirty-one names of family members of Frances Harlow embroidered on the ten-inch blocks. All the names are female except one, Joel H. Abshier, her grandson and the only child of her daughter, Juda Joanna Harlow Abshier. Mrs. Harlow's name appears in the center with the notation "Pieced by Grandma Harlow Age 83." Her daughters' blocks are immediately surrounding hers. Then come the granddaughters and great-granddaughters, each grouped near their own mother's name. The names were written by one person, and all are embroidered with white thread in a stem stitch. The quilt is hand pieced and hand quilted in diagonal lines.

The quilt represents a definite time in the history of the family, which continued to grow after the date of the quilt. Many members do not appear on the quilt but do appear on a genealogical family tree.

Frances Burris Tandy was born near Hopkinsville, Kentucky, in 1815. She married Mahlon Harlow on August 19, 1835, in Lafayette County, Missouri, and they had six children born between 1836 and 1848. In 1850 they started West

with the gold fields of California as their goal. Their journey became particularly difficult when they reached the Salt Lake. They were obliged to winter over in Mormon country because the grass along the route for the livestock had been burned. However, when the Mormons tried to impose a tax on the use of their land, they were forced to leave their temporary camp during the winter and move on toward Oregon. Settling first in Yamhill County where their daughter Juda Joanna was born in July, they moved to Lane County later in 1851.

Frances Harlow and her extended family were active members of their community. Their cabin was the organizing site for the Willamette Forks Baptist Church of Jesus Christ, the forerunner of the First Baptist Church of Eugene. Frances and Mahlon Harlow, along with her mother, Sarah Tandy, and her brothers William and Robert Tandy, Joseph Meador, and Mrs. Sarah Benson were the chartering members on July 1, 1852. On the recent 140th anniversary of the church, the congregation was gratified to discover their founder's treasured quilt at the Lane County Historical Museum.

Detail inscribed, "Pieced by Grandma Harlow Age 83"

The Harlow family played a part in the story of the Lost Wagon Train of 1853. Frances Harlow was one who rushed to get supplies organized to send to the stranded emigrants.

The Harlows eventually had ten children. Names of their sons show the tendency in the nineteenth century to name sons after famous men. Their first and second sons were Anderson Jackson and Henry Clay. Their tenth and last child was Mahlon Hall Harlow, Junior.

Full view of Harlow Album Quilt

PART TWO
1851 — 1855

1851–1855

TRAIL

Beginning of commercialism with Indians and trappers operating ferries, bridges, and supply stations, guidebooks available.

Experienced guides or husbands who knew Trail and western climate conditions.

Travel time shortened by one month.

More extended families going or there to receive arriving families.

Wagon trains larger, bringing more supplies and animals.

Food and water supplies often very limited.

Illnesses and disease become major problems.

QUILTS

Of the twenty-eight quilts:
 Thirteen were quilted when came.
 Twelve quilted after.
 One pieced while on trail.
 One not finished.
 One unknown.

Span of time represented by quilts 1830–1900

Number of quilts by year (family):
 1851: 5 (4)
 1852: 13 (10)
 1853: 6 (5)
 1854: 1 (1)
 1855: 0

Categories of quilts:
 Appliquéd: Ten
 Pieced: Twenty-one
 Crazy: Two

Themes:
 Celebration: Nine
 Migration: Twelve
 Unknown: Two

QUILT MAKERS

Age range from 10 to 64.

Three came with extended families.

One came as widow with adult children.

Eleven came with husbands.

Six came with parents.

Twelve making first migration.

Five making second migration.

One making third migration.

One making fourth migration.

Two died on the Trail.

Reasons for coming:
 Eight for economic and business opportunities.
 Eight for land.
 Two for religious opportunities.
 One for health.

One against slavery.

Four unknown.

Husbands going to the gold fields:
 Five went before bringing family.

Twelve settled in the northern Willamette Valley:
 Three in Linn County
 Two in Benton, Clackamas County, and Washington County
 One in Marion, Multnomah, and Yamhill County

Five settled in the southern Willamette Valley:
 Five in Lane County

Four settled in southern Oregon:
 Two in Douglas County
 Two in Jackson County

One settled in Washington Territory

Moved again after arriving in Oregon:
 One moved to Lincoln County.
 One moved to Multnomah (Portland).
 One moved to Umatilla County in eastern Oregon.
 One moved to Washington Territory.
 One moved to Marion County.

Role achieved in Oregon:
 Twenty-one worked to establish farm and family.
 One worked to relocate communal society.
 One organized a church.
 Two served as liaisons with Indians.
 One worked for woman's suffrage and was first woman to vote in Oregon.

QUILTING ACTIVITY

Before:
 Seven quilted between zero and five years.
 Five quilted between five and fifteen years.
 Two quilted between fifteen and twenty-five years.

After:
 Two quilted between two and five years of arriving.
 Three quilted between five and fifteen years.
 Two between fifteen and twenty-five years.
 One between twenty-five and thirty-five years.
 Four over thirty-five years.
  Annis Bonnett made her Crazy Quilt forty years later.
  Abigail Scott Duniway finished her Hexagon Quilt forty-eight years later.
  Susannah Good Morris quilted throughout her elder years.
  Grandma Zeralda Bones Stone made quilts sixty years later.

The Trail

GRADUALLY, AS THE JOURNEY PROGRESSED and knowledge about the realities of the Elephant became known, the economies of the trip began to disrupt women's lives and rob them of a sense of control and routine. Although they traveled with published guidebooks suggesting locations for encampment, by the late 1840s many were out of date or the resources of a site had been exhausted when a family sought them out. As the water and grass supplies diminished, travel days were lengthened in an effort to find the necessary water and feed. All of these obstacles created frustration among families.

The second part of the journey (from Fort Laramie to Boise) often became one of monotony and hard work. The routine of travel was established after the preparations for getting underway were accomplished: a drive of nine to twelve miles moving at an average of three miles an hour; a "nooning," or stop for dinner and rest; an afternoon of continued travel; and then the stop for the night with evening activities of rest and relaxation.

Often at the end of the day, there would be an hour or two of socialization in the form of visiting, dancing, singing, and game playing. Most of these activities by now were a combination of pain and pleasure—physical tiredness, yet the joy of accomplishment and satisfaction of achievement.

Mixed with this life of monotonous routine would be the other extreme, the moments of utter violence. Dealing with illness, whether of oneself or one's family, the death of a loved one, the accidents that would occur, the runaway wagons being pulled by frightened oxen, the complications of pregnancy and birth, and the rapid changes of weather all had to be faced and endured.

As they continued into the high plateaus and mountains toward South Pass City in Wyoming at an eight-thousand-foot elevation, the trip became more strenuous. Difficulty in finding food and potable water meant that unknown distances must be traveled. As illnesses began to set in, additional needs and requirements were placed on women's time. These changes in schedules and activities forced them to abandon some of what they valued. On occasion, to ease the work of the starving oxen, possessions were abandoned to lighten the wagon loads.

Then it might be necessary to jettison those treasures that bound the women to families and friends back East. When forced to leave behind some of her cargo, one woman penned a note inviting others to help themselves to "five good quilts."[1]

Traveling Across the Desert

When the weather was very hot, as it could be in the high plateau areas of Wyoming, Idaho, and eastern Oregon, the wagon train would travel all night and make a rest stop during the day. If this meant going through sand, they would carry as little extra water and wood as possible because of the extra weight. Night travel was particularly hard because of the difficulty of keeping track of the animals or trying to sleep with the continuous rumbling of the wagons.

At Fort Laramie, Wyoming, the first major opportunity to regroup after experiencing the Elephant of the Great Platte River Country, the scene was described as follows:

> Yesterday [May 30] being a rainy day and most trains laying by having nothing else to do, a general destruction and devastation appeared to take Place—in almost every train—I thought I had seen destruction of property but this morning beat anything I had ever seen. . . . Trunks, clothes, Matrasses [sic], Quilts, Beef, Bacon, Rice, Augers, Handsaw, Planes, Shoes, Hats, Thread, Spools, Bass [sic] Soap, Mowing sythes [sic], etc. These were thrown out yesterday by one train in order to make their loads lighter. . . .
>
> We found a number of emigrants here [at Fort Laramie]—many with broken down teams, some preparing to pack, others turning back, not being able to procure the necessaries for packing, and less able to proceed farther with their present teams. This appears to be a place of general renovating amongst travellers. Most stay a day or two for the double purpose of resting their mules and repacking their loads—Good wagons here bring from 4 to 30 dollars. Mules from 100 to 150 dollars. . . . Everything you buy cost four times as much as it is worth and every thing you sell being perhaps one tenth its value.[2]

River Crossings

During the early years (1843–1850), one of the time-consuming challenges was finding a way to cross a river. Depending on the speed of the current, the width and depth of the water, and knowledge of previous crossings, several options were available. If a current was slow and the depth and width not too much, the wagons could be pulled across by the oxen teams. To seal the cracks of the wagon against water, each wagon carried a bucket of tar, which would be carefully and liberally applied. If the current was fast, horses would be substituted for the oxen because of their greater agility. The slower, heavier animals would have to be swum across by a man going in the water with them. The young husband of Lucinda Cox Brown Spencer (Quilt A–15) died as a result of swimming the animals across the Platte River. If a river was considered too dangerous, then a raft or canoes would be built to carry each wagon across. This took time and caused significant delays in travel. If members of a party could do so, as with the Riddle family (Quilts B–6 and B–8), they would stay behind and ferry others across using their raft to earn extra money.

In later years, journeys were shortened when bridges and rafts were more readily available. These were set up by Indians or other individuals hoping to make money by charging inflated tolls.

Another advantage was gained by later wagon trains when they could employ an experienced leader who knew the route, with the best places to camp, rest, and cross the rivers and mountains. Not only did it shorten the travel time, it also helped to avoid the high-priced tolls.

Although there were other ways to find the best routes and camping places, word of mouth was always a ready source, as were the messages and notes found scribbled on dried bones and animal skeletons.

Fears

Fear of Disease. The increased number of people traveling the Trail resulted in deterioration of the water supply and an epidemic of illness and disease, especially cholera. The worst years were between 1849 and 1854. The disease had arrived on board ships from Asia and Europe to the seaports along the coasts, striking in the Midwest where it had been carried by Mississippi River steamers from New Orleans to St. Louis, then up the Missouri River. It followed the emigrants as they began their overland journeys along the Missouri and Platte rivers.

The disease and death levels were so high that President William Henry Harrison declared a national epidemic. He issued a call for ministers and religious leaders to pray for help in controlling the spread of disease. The Reverend J. H. B. Royal (Quilt B–17) included in his writings the prayer he offered in response to this request.

Fear of the Indians. The fear of Indian attacks was one of the much publicized concerns about the Trail experience. Reports were common of coming upon sites of raids and attacks, but there is no evidence that actual difficulty and brutality occurred to the families whose stories are included in this project.

Generally, the greatest difficulty came through the misunderstanding and lack of respect shown to the Indians by the whites. Several of the family histories and related stories report instances when Indians were fascinated with the young white girls. They made comments about their beauty and attractiveness. Several stories are told of how Indian men sought to trade horses for the daughters of traveling families.

In the Daniel Bayley family, the eighteen-year-old daughter Caroline was kidnapped by Indians but was rescued by a member of the train. A party of Sioux had visited their wagon train near Fort Laramie, and the chief had asked how many horses Mr. Bayley would take for his daughter. Jokingly, he replied ten. The next morning, the Indian returned with thirty horses to exchange for the girl. Not understanding Mr. Bayley's humor, the Indians became annoyed. Leaving unhappily, they later kidnapped the young girl as she wandered from camp. She was returned, only after successful negotiations by a young man, Bosh Rickner, who had traveled the West before and knew the language and culture well enough to explain the situation to the Indians.

Fear of Weather. The thunder and lightning storms along the Platte River through Nebraska and into Wyoming are some of the strongest weather occurrences anywhere. Many wagon covers were actually made like quilts, having cloth placed on either side of a rubber sheet that served to insulate and waterproof the interior. Being of soft cloth, the wagon cover was not much security in a driving rainstorm.

One pioneer, L. Jane Powell, wrote in 1900, while traveling along the Platte River, a description of the severest rain and hail storm she had ever witnessed:

Peal after peal thunder shook the ground as though it was tearing the world to pieces. The continual lightning occasionally struck the wagon tires and ran around them, presenting the appearance of great balls of fire. The wind shook the wagons until they felt as though they would upset, and the rain sifted through the heavy lined wagon covers like Oregon mist.[3]

Reports like this have shaped the perceptions of the Oregon Trail experience. Although the image of lightning circling the tires is dramatic, its actual happening is not possible.[4]

Fear for Children. Women traveling with children faced the additional challenges of keeping track of them, tending them during illness and accident, and suffering through their births and deaths. The problems of pregnancy were increased by not knowing when or where they would deliver, or what help would be available.

Six-year-old Eliza Dibble Sawtell (Quilt B–14) was bitten by a rattlesnake on the Trail, permanently injuring her leg. Lucinda Ann Leonard (Quilt B–2) was a constant worry to her family while on the Trail because of sickness. They feared she would not survive the journey, especially after being part of the Lost Wagon Train of 1853 in eastern Oregon.

For Elizabeth Currier Foster (Quilts A 3–9), the accidental death of Salita Henderson during a layover left a lasting impression. The child died of a medicine overdose, after seeing her older sister, Lucy Henderson Deady, and Elizabeth taste laudanum, which was used medicinally. She was buried in a black walnut coffin made of boards that had been a table. Elizabeth was so guilt ridden, she cut a flower from her beaded bag and placed it on the grave.

Fear of Stampede and Run-away Wagons. Another fear voiced by women like Lucinda Cox Brown Allen Spencer was the possibility of buffalo herd stampedes. In 1847 there were so many of the animals, the emigrants were aware that anything in their way would be trampled.

A greater fear occurred when the oxen pulling a wagon were spooked into a stampede. This was especially scary for the older women and children who were usually riding in the wagons. It could be caused by anything, including loose stock being driven too close to a yoked team, by the smell of water to a thirsty team, or by Indians masquerading as animals on the Trail. This risk was always present as one would never know when or how the animals might be frightened.

Elizabeth Currier Foster's beaded bag with the missing flower

Fear of Losing Role and Responsibility. As physical conditions began to deteriorate, sacrifices had to be made; and one of these often was the practice of observing the Sabbath as a day of worship. For women this sacrifice was a threat to one of their major roles, that of maintaining moral authority and religious responsibility.

At the beginning of the journey, Sunday was regarded as a day of worship and rest for some. As one woman wrote, "Men needed 'physical rest,' so they lolled around in the tents and on their blankets spread on the grass, or under the wagons out of the sunshine, seeming to realize that the 'Sabbath was made for men' . . . [Yet] women, who had only been anxious spectators of their arduous work, and not being weary in body, could not fully appreciate physical rest."[5]

For the Royal family (Quilt B–17) of Methodist ministers, the demand for a change in this practice came close to costing their lives at the Humbolt River on the Applegate Trail. Late in their journey, their supplies were extremely low. They were using borrowed oxen to pull their wagons. The leader of the train was demanding that all move forward. Mary Ann, wife of Thomas Fletcher Royal, was expecting the birth of a baby at any moment. The only physician in the party would be moving out on Sunday. All these were legitimate reasons to break tradition and travel. Mary Ann was allowed to make the decision for the family. She chose to put her trust in God. The family kept the Sabbath and survived.[6]

Detail of block

B–1

Quilt: STAR

Category: Pieced

Size: 91" x 70"

Date: circa 1830

Maker: Jane Lieb Riggs (1814–1874)

Year Over Trail: 1851

Came: As a wife, with husband, Zadoc S. Riggs, and five children

County Where Settled: Polk County, Oregon

Early fabrics and family history combine to make this a special heirloom quilt. The fabrics represent the period between 1800 and 1830, the early stages of the textile printing industry in America. There are the roller-process brown prints, the indigo-blue-and-white discharge print, the pink geometric, and the early red print with the evidence of rotting caused by the dye process. The fourteen-inch blocks are set together with three-inch sashes. At the intersections, feathered wreaths are quilted in fine detail.

Jane Lieb Riggs, who was born in Tennessee on August 21, 1814, married Zadoc S. Riggs on December 27, 1832. When they started for Oregon in 1851, Zadoc Riggs was the captain of their wagon train. Then tragedy struck, he died at the Sweetwater River crossing in Wyoming on July 5th. Their only daughter, Cynthia, died September 15 at The Dalles, Oregon. The rest of the family arrived in the Willamette Valley where they stayed with James Berry Riggs, a brother-in-law who had come the previous year.

In 1853 Jane Lieb Riggs and her four young sons staked a claim on Salt Creek in Polk County where they built a log house. In 1861 the four boys built their mother a four-room house with a double fireplace that caused the neighbors to marvel at their accomplishment.

Her life and her family have been celebrated annually at a family reunion. A newspaper clipping refers to the quilt and the reunion:

Jane Lieb Riggs

> Highlights of the dinner and the afternoon were stories connected with the antique dishes, furniture and other old possessions of the family, which the group enjoyed viewing. One of the family heirlooms of great interest was the quilt pieced by Jane Lieb Riggs and handed down to her granddaughter Jane Baxter, who in turn presented it to her great granddaughter, Jane Woods . . . on the occasion of Jane's graduation from the eighth grade last year.[7]

Full View of Star

Detail of blocks

B–2

Quilt: DELECTABLE MOUNTAINS

Category: Pieced

Size: 87" x 66½"

Date: circa 1840

Maker: Katherine Purdom (1786–?)

Year Over Trail: 1853

Sent: With daughter, Mary Purdom Leonard; her husband, Joseph Leonard; and their four children: Catherine Jane, Cyrus, Lucinda Ann, and Joseph

County Where Settled: Linn County, Oregon

The family of Lucinda Ann Leonard Worth, the granddaughter of the maker, treasure this Delectable Mountains quilt as a symbol of her survival of the Lost Wagon Train experience in 1853. As evidence of the importance of the Oregon Trail in their lives, this quilt has been cherished for five generations from the maker to the great-great-great-granddaughter.

As a nine-year-old child, Lucinda Ann suffered severe illness and exposure on the journey. According to family history, there was concern she would not survive until they reached Oregon. This is thought to have been the reason why she forbade any of her family and friends to talk or ask about her experience. This was the opposite of her older sister, Catherine, who wrote extensively for publication.*

This noncommunication is a very strong confirmation of the use of quilts as visual yet silent objects of life's passages. Their presence is known while they remain quietly stowed in a family trunk, hidden away but not thrown away.

A study of the quilt's sixteen-inch pieced blocks shows a variety of fabrics and dyes available in the mid-nineteenth century. There are fifteen different indigo-blue-and-white prints and sixteen different pink-and-brown prints in the blocks, which indicate that a significant number of fabric choices were available. Family history reveals the Purdoms originally lived along the Mississippi River in Clark County, Missouri, an area well serviced by commercial river boat transportation.

The Delectable Mountains pattern has a long tradition connected to migration through John Bunyan's allegory *Pilgrim's Progress*. The reference is, "They went then till they came to the Delectable Mountain . . . behold the gardens and orchards, the vineyards and fountains of water. . . ."8 Unfortunately, for the Leonard family, this was quite the contrast. They found cold, rain, hunger, and starvation in the mountains of central Oregon.

After finally arriving in the Willamette Valley in November, the family took up a donation land claim of 320 acres at the foot of Peterson's Butte on the Calapooia River in Linn County.

Lucinda Leonard Worth with children, Vida Ethel, born circa 1869 (left), and William Leonard, born 1865 (right)

*A copy of Catherine Jane Leonard Jones's letter describing her family's experience on the Lost Wagon Train of 1853 is in Appendix B.

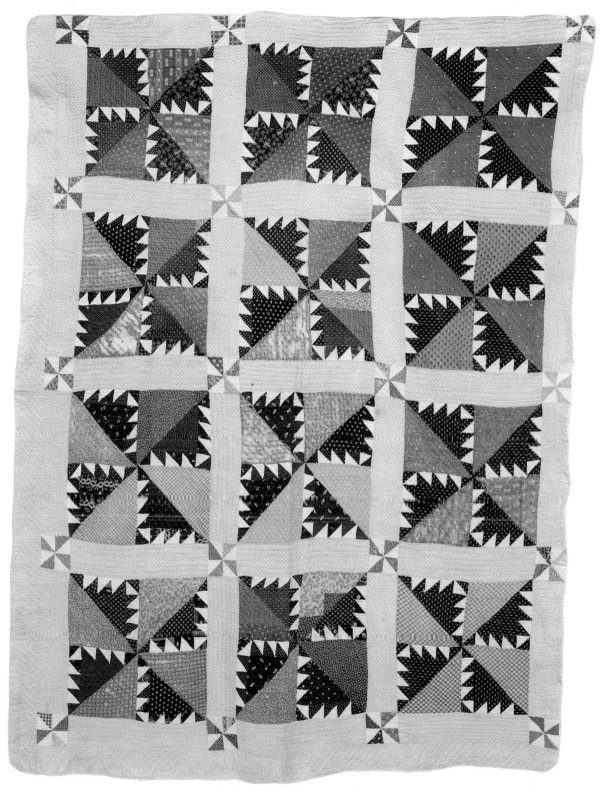

Full view of Delectable Mountains

B–3

Quilt: SETTING SUN

Category: Pieced

Size: 86″ x 71½″

Date: 1840

Maker: Margaret Hamilton Greer
(1808–1895)

Year Over Trail: 1852

Came: As a wife with husband,
James, and four of their nine children

County Where Settled: Benton
County, then Polk County,
Oregon

Detail of floral print

The accession information states
the fabrics came from the baby
dresses of George Hamilton Greer
(1836–1928), a Methodist Episcopal
minister in Oregon for fifteen years
(1860–1875). Study of the quilt reveals these to be the centers of the
sun motifs and possibly the blue and
white indigo of the sun's rays. It was
the practice of the period to use
fabrics left over from making adult
clothing for that of children. Also,
young children wore gender-neutral
clothes of the same style; so a floral
print might be expected to appear in
a boy's dress. Since they lived in
Philadelphia, a textile production
center, this family had access to the
early checked, striped, and overlaid
print.

The triangle motif across the bottom may be a ground for the sun
units, either as mountains or waves.
Triangles were used to represent
both on quilts.

James and Margaret Hamilton
Greer were born in Ireland and
immigrated in 1831. Settling in
Philadelphia, James used his trade as

a hand-weaver to work in the mills
of the area. With the advent of the
power loom and the steam process
of weaving, his job was eliminated.

Turning to farming, the family
lived in Indiana and Missouri between 1837 and 1852 when they
started for Oregon. They settled in
the King's Valley area of Benton
County. The family was actively involved with the Methodist Episcopal
Church, "cordially despising" whis-
key, gaming, and slavery. A memorial
window honors James and Margaret
Greer in the Methodist Episcopal
Church in Dallas, Oregon.[9]

Full view of Setting Sun

Detail of block

B–4

Quilt: WANDERING FOOT

Category: Pieced

Size: 85" x 67"

Date: circa 1840

Maker: Cecelia Hargrave (Unknown)

Year Over Trail: 1852

Sent: With daughter Nancy Jane Whiteaker, her husband, John, and their family

County Where Settled: Yamhill County, then Lane County, Oregon

This indigo-blue-and-white quilt, which came to Oregon as a gift, is unusual for several reasons. The pieced pattern is white on a blue ground rather than the more common blue on white. The design is one that can be either appliquéd or pieced. At this time there was a transition from mostly appliquéd to more pieced quilts.

Indigo-blue was a popular dye in the mid-nineteenth century because of its colorfastness. Prior to this, home dyes usually resulted in fugitive colors of browns, golds, and muddy greens commonly referred to as "drab." With the development of the textile industry in America, including improved dyeing and printing processes, new colorfast textiles featuring interesting design elements were produced and were readily available to quiltmakers. Having access to fabric that would retain its color was a boon to the quiltmaker.

The technical skill required to piece the thirty-one blocks is advanced. The curved edges of the narrow pieces required an experienced hand to get them to lie flat and be consistent.

The theme of migration is evident in the pieced pattern of the blocks and the triangles in the border.

The quilt was made by Mrs. Hargrave when she was living in Missouri. At the museum, its accession information states, "Mrs. Thomas Hargrave gave this to her daughter Mrs. John Whiteaker, on her 16th birthday."[10]

Nancy Jane Hargrave was born in 1828 in Indiana, and she was eighteen when her family moved from Illinois to Missouri in 1846. In 1847 she married John Whiteaker, a carpenter and cabinet maker.[11]

Leaving his wife with her parents, John Whiteaker went to the gold fields in 1851. Attracted to the West, he returned to Missouri to bring his wife to Oregon in 1852. Serving as captain of the wagon train, by October he had guided them to Yamhill County. Moving to Lane County in 1853, he staked a claim at Pleasant Hill. In 1859, he was elected the first governor of the state of Oregon and served until 1862.

The Lane County Historical Museum has two other quilts in its collection also brought West by the Whiteakers.

Full view of Wandering Foot

B–5

Quilt: WANDERING FOOT

Category: Appliqué

Date: circa 1840

Size: 87" x 72"

Maker: Member of Arsenone Patterson family

Year Over Trail: 1852

Came: With family of Cabell and Arsenone Tureman Patterson

County Where Settled: Washington County, then Lincoln County, Oregon

Although in poor condition, this red-and-green appliqué quilt illustrates a recurring pattern that appears among the Oregon Trail quilts—Wandering Foot. The pattern is important because of its connection to migration, a theme this project celebrates. The eleven-inch blocks of older fabrics indicate a date of around the 1840s. One block stands out on the quilt; it may have been an early repair. The quilt is hand stitched completely except for a replacement binding put on with sewing machine. The quilt has extensive quilting in wreaths and grid lines. There are four borders to add width to the quilt.

The quilt came from the estate of Hester Hill Coovert Rogers to the Lincoln County Historical Society. The museum has a comprehensive collection of Rogers family items. Even though the quilt is in poor condition, it is valuable as a research and material culture object.

Harriet, Hester, and Samuel Hill

Hester Hill was the daughter of Samuel and Harriet Patterson Hill. Samuel Hill was the son of Phillip and Nancy Watters Hill of Kentucky; Harriet Elizabeth was the only daughter of Cabell Adair Breckenridge Patterson of Kentucky and Arsenone Tureman. Harriet was born in 1847 in Illinois and had a brother, Corlis Patterson. The Patterson family crossed the plains by wagon in 1852 and filed a claim on November 1, 1852, on land in what is now the Tigard area of Washington County.

Harriet Patterson completed high school and attended college in Portland before joining her brother in the newly opened land for white settlers in Indian territory on North Beaver Creek in Lincoln County,

near Ona. They were the first whites to move to the Beaver Creek area. After her brother's accidental death, Harriet, alone in the wilderness, nearly lost her mind. Soon after, she married a neighboring bachelor, Samuel Hill. At the age of forty, she gave birth to her only child, Hester, on November 27, 1887.

Hester began her career as a school teacher at the age of seventeen. In 1915, at the age of twenty-eight, she married John R. Coovert. He died in 1926, leaving her a widow without children. She continued to teach in towns along the Oregon coast. In 1941 she married Jack Rogers. She died in 1966 in Arizona.

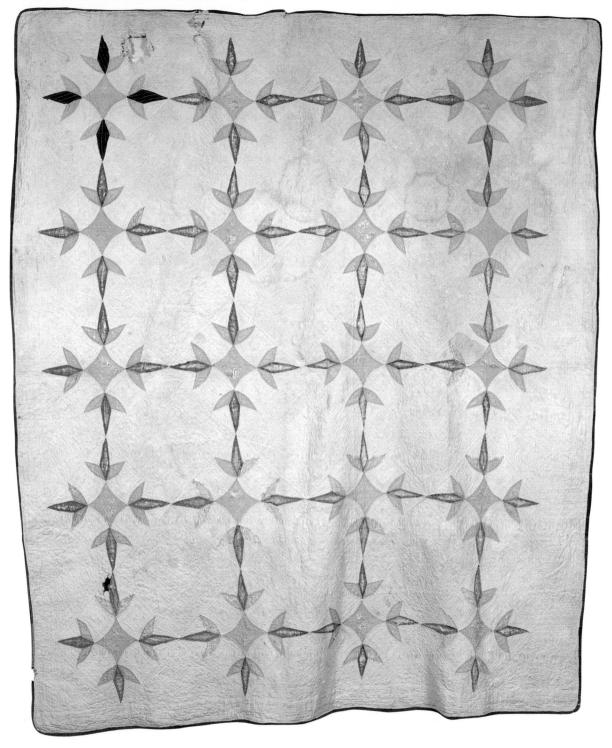

Full view of Wandering Foot

B–6

Quilt: SINGLE IRISH CHAIN

Category: Pieced

Size: 90″ x 80″

Date: 1846

Maker: Artenecia Riddle Chapman Merriman (1830–1917)

Year Over Trail: 1851

Came: As a daughter and young widow with parents, William and Maximilla Riddle, and family; and her baby son, John Chapman

County Where Settled: Douglas County, then Jackson County, Oregon

The Riddle sisters, 1902: (left to right) Artie Riddle Merriman and Mollie Riddle Beal

The Double Nine Patch set of this quilt, making the Single Irish Chain, creates a sense of movement across the surface. The quilt was hand-pieced of three-inch blocks of early blue and white fabrics which place it as perhaps the work of a young woman learning to sew.

The quilted wreaths with the grid of intersecting lines show a count of fifteen stitches per inch. This indicates that the work may have been finished later as the maker became a more talented needleworker, or that it was completed by a different, more experienced quilter.

Artenecia Riddle Merriman was born in West Liberty, Ohio, in 1830. At the age of eighteen, she married John Chapman and lived in Springfield, Illinois. He died in 1851, just a few days prior to her parents' planned departure for Oregon, leaving her a young widow and mother. She had little choice but to emigrate

with them, leaving Illinois in late May. Although traveling with her family, she had her own wagon and three teams of oxen.

An incident on her journey was vividly recalled by her brother, George W. Riddle. After a gun shot shattered the bone in the arm of a member of their train, Artenecia Chapman bravely forced the bone fragments out and dressed the wound. The patient recovered well. "I witnessed the operation and it made such an impression upon my mind that at times I can visualize the operation. My sister Artenecia was a brave girl."[12]

In 1853 Artenecia married widower William H. Merriman, a member of an 1852 wagon train, in Douglas County. They had fourteen children of their own, in addition to one each from their former marriages.

In 1857 they moved to Rogue River Valley where Artenecia became an interpreter between the government and the Indians because of her ability to speak Chinook.

Her sewing machine was the first in the Rogue Valley, producing considerable interest from the people of the area.

As an Oregon pioneer, she was one of those receiving recognition in her adopted state. Her participation and photo in an early silent promotional film *Gracie Visits the Rogue Valley* was featured at the 1915 San Francisco Exposition's Oregon Building.

For forty years after her husband's death, she celebrated her life by traveling extensively to visit her children, grandchildren, and great-grandchildren.

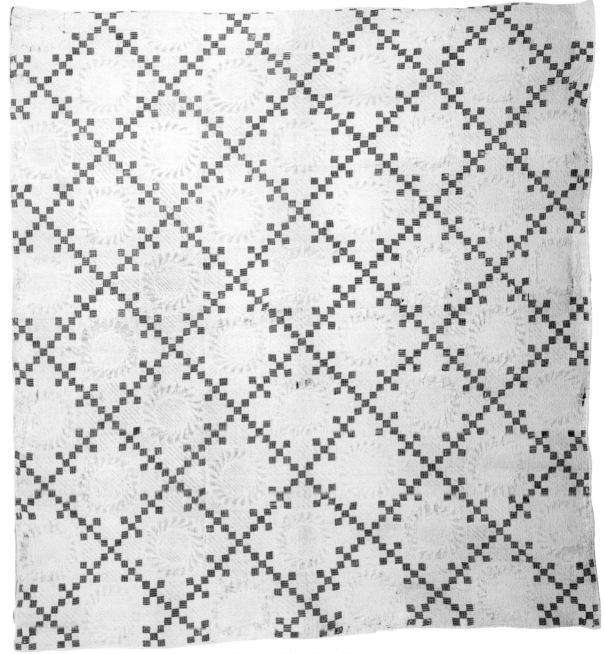

Full view of Single Irish Chain

B–7

Quilt: PEONY WITH FLYING
    GEESE BORDER

Category: Pieced and Appliqué

Size: 80″ x 78″

Date: 1848 dated

Maker: Grace Weaver (1815–1885)
    or Susanna Weaver (1787–
    1872)

Year Over Trail: 1852

Sent: With family of Hans Weaver, Jr.

County Where Settled: Douglas
    County, Oregon

Detail with "S. W. 1848" quilted

The red and green pieced and
appliquéd peonies alternate with
blocks of white stuffwork wreaths.
The pieced green-print triangles in
the border, known as Flying Geese,
are a migration motif. The way the
geese trail off two of the edges adds
a bit of whimsy and a sense of the
unknown.

The peony is a flower that often
appears in floral appliqué quilts. Its
meaning in the nineteenth century
lexicon of flowers is "healing."[13]

The quilt has the initials "S.W."
with the date "1848" on the front
above the lower right border.

Researching the family history has
been challenging because the dates
contradict, the name Susannah re-
peats through the generations, and
an incomplete copy of the history
was filed with the Douglas County
Museum of History Library in
Roseburg, Oregon.

Compiled by A. C. Seely, the
history states, "My wife has a quilt
made by Grace Weaver for her niece
Susannah (Hall) Weaver. A beautiful
piece of very complicated needle
work, hand made."

The history also states that Susannah Weaver Hall was the only
daughter born to Hans Weaver, Jr.,
and Harriet Bigham Weaver on July
19, 1842, in Washington County,
Illinois. The parents had married

August 26, 1841, in Guernsey
County, Ohio. They migrated to Illinois in 1843. The family came across
the plains in 1852 or 1853. Her
father objected to her marriage, Susannah being his only daughter; so
she left home to marry the man of
her choice, John Hall. The quilt
passed through her family until it
was donated to the museum in
1969.

In contradiction, the accession re-
cord states, "made for Susannah
Weaver, b. 1818 in Philadelphia, by
Grace Weaver, b. 1814 in Ireland."
There is no information about their
lives or their deaths.[14]

This is a beautiful, richly decorated masterpiece that probably took
months, if not years, to complete.
Women without the responsibility of
managing a home and family could
spend countless hours focusing on
their needlework. Young single
women did piecing and quilting for
hope chests prior to marriage, and
maiden aunts made quilts for other
family members. The quilt could
have been a gift for the young niece
Grace would rarely see because of
the traditions of leave-taking and
family migrations. Or an older
woman who had nine adult sons and

Susannah Weaver Hall

daughters could have made the quilt
for a granddaughter who was her
namesake; the S.W. could refer to
Susanna Cleland Weaver. The name
and date generally refer to the
woman who made the quilt and the
date it was completed. The style fits
with the quilts being made at this
mid-nineteenth century period in
Ohio quiltmaking.

Full view of Peony with Flying Geese Border

B–8

Quilt: BIRDS IN FLIGHT VARIA-
TION

Category: Pieced

Size: 86½" x 76"

Date: circa 1850

Maker: Member of Maximilla Riddle
Family

Year Over Trail: 1851

Came: As a wife with William
Riddle; three daughters, including
Artenecia and her baby, Isabella,
Anna; four sons, William, Abner,
John, F. Stilley; her half-sister,
Lucinda McGill, age forty-five;
and an orphaned niece, Anna
Hall, age eleven.

County Where Settled: Douglas
County, Oregon

Full view of Birds in Flight Variation

Triangles in quilts have long
represented birds in flight, and thus
the pattern name connects to a
migration and outdoor theme. The
forty-two pieced blocks each contain
forty-nine triangles for over two
thousand pieces hand-stitched
together. The many varieties of
brown, yellow, and blue fabrics date
from the 1840s and earlier. The
placement of the butterscotch-yellow
prints in the four corners, and the
single strip of indigo-blue-and-white
triangles in the center show the
thought the maker put in the
placement of her blocks.

There is a possibility the quilt was
pieced on the Trail because of the
many small triangles and the large
number of women traveling together
in the Riddle family.

The family came over the Trail in
1851 with a large party of forty men
and a few women. They were lured
to Oregon by the high praise of the
territory from a respected Illinois
neighbor, Isaac Constant, who had
returned from the Northwest. Their
party came with three wagons, each
drawn by three yoke of oxen; one

large carriage pulled by four horses,
which they abandoned along the
Platte River; and forty head of
cattle, cows, and heifers.

They chose the Applegate Trail,
the southern route into Oregon
across Utah and Nevada. Following
the recommendation of a friend,
they settled one of the first claims on
Cow Creek in southern Douglas
County.

This was the home of the Cow
Creek Indians with whom the extended family had excellent relations.
Because of this, the mother, Maximilla, once negotiated with them a
cease-fire during a time of con-
flict. In 1855, while under the threat
of attack from the Indians and
grieving from the death of her
daughter Clara whom she wanted to
bury in safety, Maximilla was able to

bring the threatening group of
Indians together with the neighbors
by riding alone to the Indians' camp
and convincing them to talk.
Respect was re-established with the
local Indians, and nothing was
destroyed in the white neighbors'
homes that they deserted for safety.

Maximilla Riddle demonstrated
her commitment to help build her
home and community by
accompanying her two sons, Abner
and George, ages twelve and
fourteen, on trips to Portland in the
summers of 1852–1854. They went
by wagon to purchase agricultural
equipment, especially plows, to sell
in southern Oregon. The three
camped out along the four-hundred-
mile round trip.[15]

B–9

Quilt: ROAD TO CALIFORNIA

Category: Pieced

Size: 73" x 63"

Date: circa 1850

Maker: Nancy Gates Ensley Drain
   (1817–1893)

Year Over Trail: 1852

Came: As a wife with husband,
   Charles Drain, and family

County Where Settled: Marion
   County, then Douglas County,
   Oregon

Full view of Road to California

Road to California[16] was most likely a deliberate choice of pattern for the indigo-blue-and-white nine-inch blocks of this quilt. The pieced triangles represent the "wandering" of Charles Drain who left his wife and family in Indiana in 1850 to go to the gold fields, returning in 1851.

Nancy Gates Ensley was born in Venango County, Pennsylvania, on May 20, 1817, to John and Catherine Gates Ensley. The family moved to Bartholomew County, Indiana, in 1824 where she later married Charles Drain, an orphan from the age of five. After their marriage, they moved to Van Buren County, Iowa, where he farmed.

In 1850 and 1851 he was in the California gold fields mining and working in a mercantile business. He returned to the Midwest via Panama and, impressed with the mild climate of the Pacific Coast, he brought his family to Oregon in 1852.

They settled for eight years on a farm in Marion County, where he was elected to the territorial council and state senate.

In 1860 the family moved to Douglas County where they acquired over 1,700 acres of land. In 1871 he donated land to the Oregon and California Railroad Company for a depot and laid out the town of Drain.

John and Nancy Drain celebrated their fiftieth wedding anniversary in 1889. Nancy Drain was the key figure in a piece of Oregon's early pioneer lore as the owner of a darning needle, the only one in the valley. The other key figure was Aaron Meier, founder of the Meier and Frank Department Store, another Oregon tradition.*

*An account of the darning needle story is in Appendix B.

Charles Drain and Nancy Gates Ensley Drain

Detail of pair of doves on perch

B–10

Quilt: ROSE VARIATION

Category: Appliqué

Size: 90″ x 90″

Date: circa 1850

Maker: Zeralda Carpenter Bones Stone (1822–1914)

Year Over Trail: 1853

Came: As a wife with second husband, Samuel Stone, and two children

County Where Settled: Polk County, Oregon

This Rose Variation appliqué quilt is now thought to have an earlier date than the previously assigned date of circa 1880. Recent research has brought forth new information on dating fabrics and styles of quilts. The red and green colors of the twenty-four-inch blocks are mid-nineteenth century. The construction of the sewing thread appears to be wrapped, as were the earlier threads. The randomly placed quilting designs were more common in the mid-century than later. The designs of this quilt are different from the large number of Zeralda Stone's other quilts. The unique border of pairs of doves on perches suggests the possibility of a wedding quilt.

Zeralda Carpenter, born in Cass County, Missouri, in 1822, married John Bones on March 1, 1844. They had two children, Sarah Jane born in 1845 and John W. born in 1849. After John Bones died in 1849, she married Samuel Stone on December 22, 1851, and they came over the plains in 1853.

Settling in Polk County near Buell, they registered Donation Land Claim Number 3611 on March 17, 1854.[17] Two of their three children died in infancy, with the third, Thomas Buford, born September 1, 1857.

Grandma Stone, as she has been referred to by people who know her quilts, was an active member of her community and was one of fourteen organizers of the Christian Church near Sheridan. She also provided a home for eleven motherless children and served as a comforter and an aid to the sick and needy.

She is an excellent example of the few women who came relatively early to Oregon, established a farm, worked to serve her community, and either stayed with quilting or returned to it later in life. Quilting offered her satisfaction.

Her quilts have become a celebration of life. According to her great-grandson, Silas E. Starr, she made many quilts that she gave to relatives and friends. In 1967 he donated at least seventeen of them, representing a long career of quilt-making, to the Oregon Historical Society. It has been noted that she never wore glasses although she made quilts continuously over a seventy-year period.

Grandma Zerelda Carpenter Bones Stone

Full view of Rose Variation

B–11

Quilt: OREGON ROSE

Category: Appliqué

Size: 88½" x 84"

Date: 1851

Makers: Friends, neighbors, and relatives of the Robbins family

Year Over Trail: 1852

Sent: With Jacob and Sarah Robbins and their nine children; his cousin Nathaniel and Nancy Robbins, with five single children and three married children and spouses

County Where Settled: Marion County, Oregon

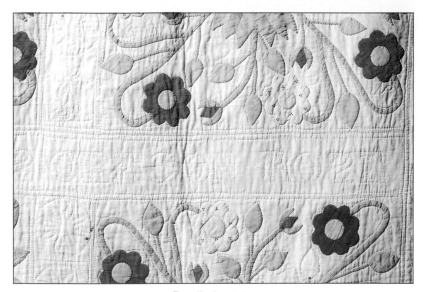

Detail of quilting

This red and green appliqué is the classic Oregon Trail quilt. It was made for the Robbins family as they prepared to leave for Oregon. Inscribed on the quilt are "Jacob and Sarah Oregon Rose!" the date "1851" and the initials "R," "S," and two "N's." Other designs randomly placed and quilted are wheels, hearts, and grapevines. The theme is migration, in the pattern name and quilting designs.

Jacob Robbins (1809–1896) and Sarah Spilman (1812–1865), natives of Kentucky, were married March 23, 1833, in Decatur County, Indiana, and became the parents of nine children. A tenth was born in Oregon in 1857.

Because of a well-written family history, the story of their migration and the extended Robbins family in Oregon is quite complete. One reason why they wanted to migrate was the large number of people in Decatur County with the last name of Robbins. According to the history, this Jacob was called "Little Toe Jake," "Oregon Jake," and "Redhouse Jake."[18] He and his wife were encouraged to make the move West by his cousin. They sold their farm and gathered the necessary

equipment and supplies, with Sarah and her helpers quickly making woolen clothing and bedding for the journey.

As the family traveled westward, they often experienced bad weather, swarms of bugs, lack of timber, lost or stampeding livestock, insufficient food, and bad water. The water may have been the cause of cholera, the highly infectious illness that ultimately resulted in the deaths of three of Nathaniel Robbins's daughters and one son-in-law. Reference is made to the girls being buried together on a mattress in a wagon box covered with quilts and blankets.[19]

Death struck the Jacob Robbins family when two of their sons died: Aaron, age five, at the Sandy River near the end of the Trail, and Theodore, age eight, just after they had arrived at Sam Barlow's place and their destination near Oregon City.

After spending the winter in a large two-story house in Linn City, Oregon, Jacob Robbins filed a claim on land in Marion County and later on Salem Prairie. In the early 1860s, they moved to the Mollala area where Sarah Robbins died on Christmas Day 1865.

Sarah Spilman Robbins (1812–1865)

Jacob Robbins (1809–1896)

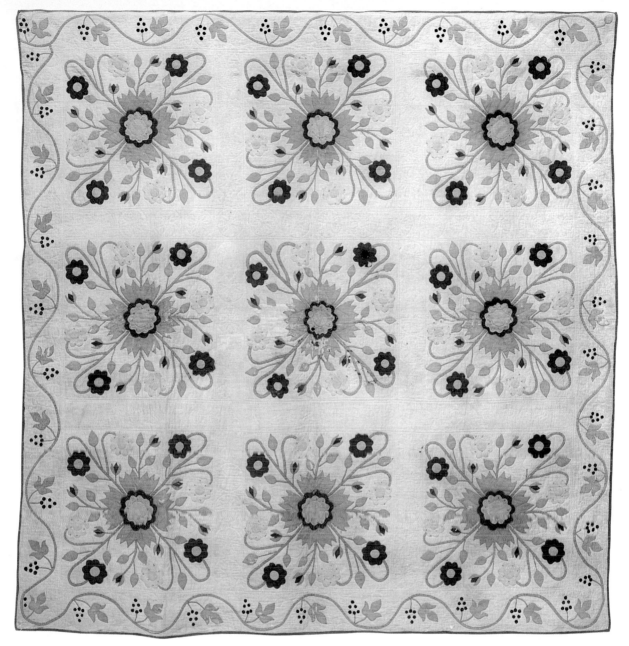

Full view of Oregon Rose

B–12

Quilt: TULIP

Category: Appliqué

Size: 85½" x 77"

Date: 1851–1852

Maker: Relatives and friends of Lucinda Powell Propst (1817–1852)

Year Over Trail: 1852

Sent: With family of Anthony Propst and Lucinda Powell Propst, their five children, and nephew Franklin Propst

County Where Settled: Both parents died; children raised by uncles in Benton and Linn counties, Oregon

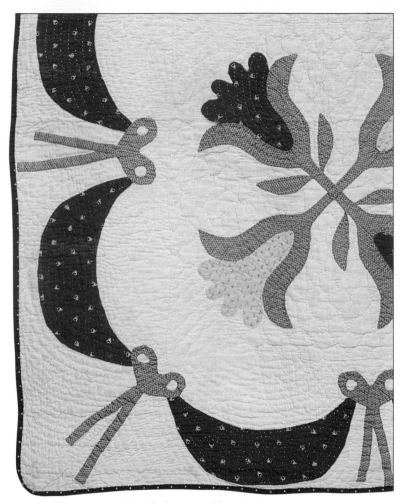

Detail of swag and bow border

This quilt has been a treasured heirloom ever since the fateful journey of the Propst family. It was handed down to Wanita Propst Haugen when she was a child by her great-grandfather, John Wesley Propst, the eldest orphaned child of Lucinda Powell Propst.[20]

Its fabrics of soft-shaded red, yellow, and green are those of the 1840s. The appliquéd tulip in the lexicon of symbols means "renown, fame, spring, and dreaminess,"[21] all possible references by friends to a woman who "dreamed" of being with her family and brothers in the Northwest. The simple swag border on three sides with the primitive bow appliqué adds an element of delight.

Lucinda was the fifth daughter of Joseph and Sarah Alkire Powell, born February 19, 1817, in Champaign County, Ohio. The family moved to Sugar Grove, Menard County, Illinois, in 1825. She married Anthony Propst in 1836, and they became the parents of six children born between 1837 and 1849 (a daughter, Sarah, died at age seven).

Eager to join her parents and brothers John, Noah, and Alfred and their families who had migrated in 1851, Lucinda persuaded her husband to make the journey to Oregon. They started with an outfit of two wagons, nine yoke of oxen, a two-horse light wagon, and thirteen head of cattle. Among their personal items was this quilt.

The journey went well until they reached the Blue Mountains in eastern Oregon. There the dream of joining her family ended when she died and was buried August 19, 1852, on Butter Creek near Echo in Umatilla County. An official historical marker is on the former site of her grave along the Trail on the Madison donation-land-claim ranch.

Later, while crossing the Cascade Mountains, Anthony Propst became ill and died at Philip Foster's place in Clackamas County.* The five children were taken to their Powell uncles where they were raised in the Willamette Valley's Benton and Linn counties.[22]

*A diary entry describing the circumstances of his death is included in Appendix B.

Full view of Tulip

B–13

Quilt: WANDERING FOOT

Category: Pieced

Size: 82" x 74"

Date: 1852

Maker: Almedia Grimsley Morris (1826–1912)

Year Over Trail: 1851

Came: As a wife with husband, Joseph Hooker Morris, and one daughter

County Where Settled: Benton County, Oregon

Detail of fabric and quilting

The thirteen pieced blocks of indigo-blue-and-white fabric with some additional yellow are fifteen and one-half inches in size. The solid blocks are made of fabric brought as a bolt over the Trail and also used for baby clothes for the infant born in April 1852. Originally the color of this fabric was purple, but it has turned brown over the years. The instability of color, common at that time in fabrics of this hue, was caused by exposure to heat and light. The lines of elbow quilting are spaced five-eighths of an inch apart in the solid blocks. The quilting in the pieced blocks echoes that of the pattern. There is a two-inch border on all sides of the quilt.

The quilt was completed in the winter of 1852 in Oregon City after the family crossed the plains from Iowa in 1851. Knowing that the fabric had been bought for baby clothes and understanding the significance of the Wandering Foot to the theme of migration, the conclusion is that this quilt was pieced on the Trail as the couple moved westward.

Almedia Grimsley and Joseph Hooker Morris were married in 1847 in Washington County, Iowa. They arrived in Oregon in November 1851 with one daughter. Her parents, John and Mary Scott Grimsley, had migrated in November 1847. Her father was a preacher. The young couple stayed with the Grimsleys that first winter, and their daughter Sarah was born in April 1852. By November of that year, they had secured a claim in Benton County.

The quilt has been a treasured heirloom of Leona Donaldson Rink, Almedia's great-granddaughter, and Honora Dallas, her great-great-granddaughter.

Almedia Grimsley Morris

Full view of Wandering Foot

B–14

Quilt: DOUBLE NINE PATCH

Category: Pieced

Size: 83″ x 74″

Date: 1856

Maker: Eliza Emily Dibble Sawtell (1846–1927)

Year Over Trail: 1852

Came: As a child with parents, Horace and Julia Ann Sturges Dibble, and two brothers

County Where Settled: Clackamas County, Oregon

The small three and one-half-inch blocks are grouped in larger squares of nine blocks each, creating the Double Nine Patch pattern. It is a traditional pattern used for young children to learn simple running stitches in needlework. Such was the case with this work done when Eliza Emily Dibble was ten years old.

The blocks are predominantly indigo-blue-and-white prints of the mid-nineteenth century. The center of each small block is a different print, which serves to create a secondary design of lines across the surface.

In setting the blocks together, there appears to have been a conscious decision by the maker to place the ones with all the same fabrics near the center of the quilt. The blocks on the edges tend to have a variety of blue-and-white prints in each one.

The quilting designs in the solid blocks are wreath patterns, some with double lines of grid work and others with feathers. Again, tradition has it that sometimes these early piecing projects, when completed, would be celebrated by having older adults assist in quilting.[23] This may well have been the work of adult women to support the young girl's early piecing effort.

Detail of fabric and quilting

According to family history, Eliza was born in Van Buren County, Iowa, on May 25, 1846. She was six years old when her family left for Oregon.

On the Trail, she was bitten on her leg by a rattlesnake. As a result, her leg never developed correctly and limited her activity, so she became an excellent seamstress. Perhaps this was an added reason why her early patchwork was encouraged by the older women in her family.

She married Alfred Sawtell on March 23, 1869, and had one daughter, Iva May. Sawtell owned and operated the Teasel Ranch on Sawtell Road. He hired Chinese workers to plant, cultivate, and harvest the teasel that was used to raise the nap on the woolen blankets woven in the area's mills.[24]

Eliza Emily Dibble Sawtell

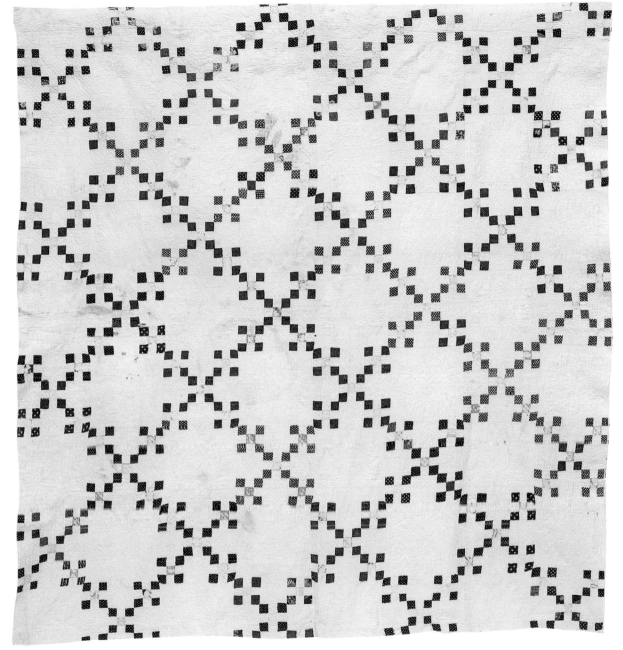

Full view of Double Nine Patch

B–15

Quilt: RUNNING SQUARES

Category: Pieced

Size: 81" x 77"

Date: circa 1860

Maker: Emma Wagner Giesy (1835–1882)

Year Over Trail: 1853

Came: As the only woman in a party of ten Bethel, Missouri, scouts to find an Oregon site for their communal society

County Where Settled: Willapa, Washington Territory, later Marion County, Oregon

This wool quilt, a treasure from the Aurora Colony, is an outstanding example of life within the communal society in Marion County of the Willamette Valley between 1855 and 1877.

The pieced quilt of eight-and-three-quarter-inch blocks is made of woolen fabric totally produced in the communal society. The wool for fabric and batt was from sheep raised by the colony. The rich colors were natural dyes of black, red from madder root, and green from the area's peach leaves.

The quilting pattern is a unique arrangement, a possible variation on the traditional elbow/fan. The parallel lines come together forming a deep V shape. The eight-and-one-half-inch border has a zig-zag arrangement of straight lines placed one and one-quarter inches apart.

The quilt is marked with the cross-stitched initials "C. G." in the same quilting thread. The marking appears in the middle of one of the solid red blocks near the bottom of the quilt. Its casual placement suggests perhaps a laundry marking, needed for purposes of doing communal laundry.

Detail of fabric and quilting

Emma Wagner Giesy was born in 1835. In 1853, when her young husband, Christian Giesy, was chosen to lead a party of scouts, she would not be left behind, reportedly saying, "What trials of the wilderness trail you face I will face, what privations and dangers you face I will face."

Arriving in the West in October of 1853, they wintered at the Puget Sound Military Post at Fort Steilacoom, Washington Territory. It was there that Emma Giesy gave birth to her first son, Andrew Jackson Giesy, in October.

The following spring, Christian Giesy and some others of the party staked claims in the Willapa Valley along the Willapa River and Bay. There the Giesys lived in a canvas-covered log house. This was the site that Dr. Keil rejected once he got to Oregon as too isolated and moved instead to the Aurora location.[25] Christian Giesy drowned in 1857 while crossing the bay. Seven months later, Christian Giesy, Jr., was born. Emma Wagner Giesy brought her two sons to Aurora in 1861.[26]

Full view of Running Squares

B-16

Quilt: HOVERING HAWKS AND
    PEONIES

Category: Pieced and Appliqué

Size: 69½" x 68"

Date: circa 1865

Maker: Sarah Amanda Ann
    Hazelton Gilfrey (1844–1884)

Year Over Trail: 1850

Came: As a daughter with parents,
    Royal and Mary Ann Hazelton,
    and family

County Where Settled: Lane County,
    Oregon

Detail of piecing

This predominantly red and green quilt celebrates nature and the outdoors and, very likely, the maker's Trail experience, in a mixture of large pieced and appliquéd blocks measuring eighteen inches square. Although the motifs of pieced triangles and peonies and themes of nature and migration are common in nineteenth-century quilts, this design is original.

The carefully placed dark triangles create the effect of dark Hovering Hawks above the brown earth in three blocks and the blue river in the other two. The peony again has the meaning of "healing" in the nineteenth-century floral lexicon. After a Trail experience, the pioneers truly needed healing, rest, and recovery. The quilting patterns include feathers in the peony blocks and on the borders. The borders match on opposite sides of the quilt, giving variety and interest to the original interpretation of the appliquéd red blooms.

Sarah Amanda Ann Hazelton Gilfrey was born in Green County,

Missouri, in 1844 to Royal and Mary Ann Reynolds Hazelton. Her father went to the gold fields in 1849. Unsuccessful in mining, he learned of opportunities in the West; so in 1850 he and his family joined a train where he served as wagon repairman. They first settled west of Skinners Butte in what is now Eugene. A year later they moved twenty miles south to Hazelton Creek where he built a sawmill and gristmill and created the village of Royal.

Family history relates that while Royal Hazelton was gone, a peddler offered Mary Ann a bolt of silk material. Eager to have the fabric and short of cash, she traded a pig

to get the cloth. After that, Hazelton Creek was called Silk Creek.[27]

Sarah married George Gilfrey and had one daughter, Nellie, before she died in 1884.

The quilt, part of the Lane County Historical Museum collection, was a focal point of a national traveling exhibit entitled "Webfoots and Bunchgrassers: Folk Art of the Oregon Country" in 1980, part of the continuing celebration of Oregon pioneer women.

Full view of Hovering Hawks and Peonies

B–17

Quilt: ROYAL PRESENTATION
QUILT

Category: Pieced

Size: 87" x 75½"

Date: 1868

Makers: Women and daughters of
the Cowlitz Circuit of the Methodist Episcopal Church in
Washington Territory

Made for: The Reverend J. H. B. and
Mrs. Emily Julia Cornell Royal

Year Over Trail: 1852

Came: Reverend J. H. B. Royal came
with his extended family

County Where Settled: Jackson
County, Douglas County,
Multnomah County, Oregon;
Cowlitz County, Lewis County,
Klickitat County, Washington Ter-
ritory; Multnomah County,
Marion County, Oregon

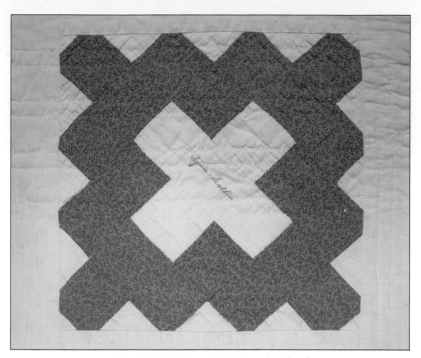

Detail with "Agnes Catlin" embroidered

This album quilt, the quintessen-
tial research experience for a quilt
historian, was presented to the Reverend James Henry Bascom Royal at
the time of his second marriage, to
Emma Julia Cornell in 1868. The
quilt with forty-one names was given
to the Eastern Washington Historical Society with the documentation
that it was "made by the Women of
Claquato Methodist Church in 1869
for wedding gift to Mrs. J. H. B.
Royal, 19 year old bride of their
pastor."[28]

Beginning the research by identifying the site and county through a
historical atlas, seeking the history of
the minister through Methodist
Church archives at Willamette University in Salem, Oregon, and
Olympia, Washington, reading *The
Royal Way West, Volume II,* and
working with Ruth Stoller, a noted
authority on the history of Methodism in the Northwest, made it

possible to connect the quilt to one
of the richest histories about an
extended family's experience in migration, settlement, and development
of the Methodist Episcopal Church
in the Northwest.

The quilt was made by mothers
and daughters along the Cowlitz
Circuit in Cowlitz County, Washington Territory, where the Reverend
J. H. B. Royal served in 1855–56
and 1866–67. Prior to having
churches and parsonages, Methodist
ministers, called circuit riders, served
their faithful by traveling through an
area on horseback to hold meetings
and classes in people's homes. In this
case, The Reverend Mr. Royal would
travel on land by foot and on water
by boat serving the areas along the
Columbia and Cowlitz rivers of Oak
Point, Rock Point, Kalama Prairie,
and later Freeport (Catlin) and
Monticello. In 1869 he went to
serve the Claquato church in Lewis
County for a year.

Many of the quiltmakers were
daughters of prominent citizens of
the area recognized for settling the
territory and helping to develop a
governmental system. Names like
Catlin and Huntington appear often
in the history of the region. Several
of the names, Laffy, Clark, and
Washburn, were identified as being
directly involved with supporting the
church in their community.[29]

The minister was deservedly popular and accomplished much good in
spite of the physical handicaps of
impaired vision and hearing resulting from having had measles as a
baby.

The Reverend Mr. Royal had
come to Oregon with his extended
family at age twenty-three in 1853.
His father, three sons, and one son-
in-law were all Methodist ministers
coming to help establish the church
in Oregon. The published materials
about their journey and their lives
are extensive.

Full view of Royal Presentation Quilt

The Reverend Mr. Royal was married to Carrie A. Hall in 1858, and they had two sons before her death in 1866. Two years later he married Emma Jane Cornell, daughter of William and Emily Castle Cornell, and they had two daughters. She assisted him in his ministry until blindness forced him to retire in 1875. They then lived in Salem and Portland, where his extended family could help them. Much loved and respected, he died in 1910.

The Reverend J. H. B. Royal seated with his wife, Emily Jane, behind him at Royal family gathering, circa 1900.

B–18

Quilt: PIECED STAR

Category: Pieced

Size: 87" x 87"

Date: circa 1869

Maker: Mary Whitley Gilmour
(1788–1877)

Year Over Trail: 1852

Came: As a widow with her daughter and son-in-law, George and Mary Ellen Gilmour Crawford, and their family

County Where Settled: Linn County, Oregon

Mary Whitley Gilmour

This richly quilted, vividly colored masterpiece quilt is part of the large collection at the Daughters of the American Revolution Museum in Washington, D.C. It is a tribute to a pioneer woman who made the journey at age sixty-four after her husband had passed away. She is the oldest woman to come over the Trail to be noted in this project. Her life spanned the period from the Kentucky frontier to the Oregon frontier.

The quilt is composed of nine hand-pieced twenty-four-inch stars. The fabric colors are typical of the mid-nineteenth century: cheddar, blue, and green with a pink, a white, and a brown print. There is a possibility that the piecing was done earlier, as with some of the other quilts of the study.

Four large white blocks of twenty-four inches contain large, quilted wreaths and leaves, while twelve small, white twelve-inch squares have a pineapple or flower sprig quilted in each. There are also grids of diagonal parallel lines.

The quilting thread is a six-ply cotton, and the binding is machine stitched. Both corroborate the date of completion of circa 1869.[30]

Mary Whitley Gilmour was born in 1788 in Lincoln County, Kentucky, to Colonel William and Esther Fuller Whitley. Her birthplace, the first brick house in the state, is now a registered early-Kentucky landmark and contains her portrait painted in the later years of her life. Built by her father in 1786, the home is called Sportsman Hill. It was the center of Kentucky political activity until the first legislature convened at Danville following Kentucky's separation from Virginia. Colonel Whitley, a Revolutionary War patriot, represented his county at the first convention.

Mary Whitley married Dr. James Gilmour in 1814, and they had ten children. In 1833 they moved to Illinois. After his death, she came to Oregon with her daughter and family, settling in Linn County in the Willamette Valley. Her son-in-law, George Crawford, became active in Oregon politics, serving two terms in the Oregon legislature.

According to the documentation, Mrs. Gilmour was a skilled needlewoman. A neighbor, Mrs. James McKnight, engaged her to piece several quilts for her. This quilt was given by Mrs. McKnight to her daughter, Roma Jane McKnight.

Full view of Pieced Star

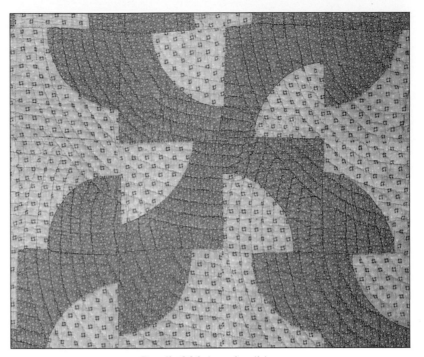

Detail of fabric and quilting

B-19

Quilt: OREGON TRAIL

Category: Pieced

Size: 69" x 67"

Date: circa 1880

Maker: Julia Ann Sturges Dibble
   (1825–1904)

Year Over Trail: 1852

Came: As a wife with husband,
   Horace, and three children

County Where Settled: Clackamas
   County

This pattern, called Oregon Trail, is one of the many variations grouped under the general name of Drunkard's Path. The design is made by cutting a curved piece from the corner of a square and then exchanging them in the piecing process. The way the seven-inch blocks are placed determines the trail of the design across the quilt surface.

The variation was identified as a pattern name by Carlie Sexton, a mail-order pattern source from Wheaton, Illinois, in the 1920s and 1930s. She published pamphlets featuring old-fashioned designs from yesterday's quilts.[31]

The binding fabric is an interesting double-pink print of small figures chasing other small figures. It appears to be the original binding and dates after 1875.[32]

Julia Ann Sturges Dibble was born in New York, January 3, 1825,

Julia Ann Sturges Dibble

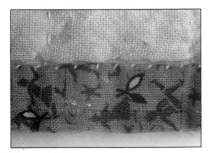

Detail of double pink fabric binding, circa 1880

the daughter of Aaron Burr and Eliza Hougland Sturges. Moving to Iowa, she married Horace Dibble July 1, 1845. They came West in 1852 with their three small children, including Eliza Emily Dibble, the maker of quilt B-14.

In 1856 for their Oregon house, Horace Dibble hired a builder to construct a salt-box house reminis-

cent of the homes from his New England boyhood. The work took three years, and the cost of the labor for the six-room house of handmade bricks and hand-planed lumber was 320 acres of land.

In her later years, Julia Ann Dibble used the small south bedroom for her bedroom-sitting room.

The property now houses the museum of the Mollala Area Historical Society where quilts, including the Wright, Robbins, and Dibble ones in this survey are exhibited each Mother's Day weekend.[33]

Dibble house, Molalla, Oregon

Full view of Oregon Trail

B-20

Quilt: FLORAL

Category: Appliqué

Size: 86″ x 74″

Date: 1875–1900

Maker: Susannah Good Morris
(1822–1915)

Year Over Trail: 1851

Came: As a wife with husband,
Eliam S. Morris, and their five
children

County Where Settled: Yamhill
County, Oregon

Susannah Good Morris

The thirty-five-inch size of the
block is an example of the scale of
things in this woman's life. She and
several members of her family lived
into their nineties, with one uncle
living to 111 years. Her home had
rooms large enough to hold a total
of ten double beds. The garden was
planted with shrubs and vines that
grew and grew. One ninety-year-old
grape vine was over 240 feet long.
On Sundays she would faithfully
prepare dinner for an average of
thirty-five to forty people.

The quilt's intricate appliqué work
shows excellent craftsmanship, except
for quilting thread knots showing
on the top of the quilt. These may
indicate the work of two different
people or the work of the same person done at two different periods of
her life.

Susannah Good was born in Missouri in 1822. In March 1839 in
Wisconsin she married Eliam S.
Morris, who was a native of Pennsylvania. They had eleven children
born between 1840 and 1858. The

family settled in Yamhill County and
purchased Donation Land Claim
Number 1330 for five hundred dollars. The Yamhill County Museum
has a supply trunk brought across
the plains and a bed made soon after
the family arrived. In 1951 the Morris family celebrated the farm's
centennial.

Dr. Henry Morris of Salem,
Oregon, described his grandmother's
quilting as follows:

My grandmother pieced quilts
and quilted them. She always
had a quilt in the quilting
frame. I think every grandchild
has a quilt that she quilted especially for them. Money would

not buy mine. My personal impression is that she had pieced
and quilted well over a hundred
quilts; perhaps all of which she
gave away with the exception of
those that she used in the house.
That was no small number, as I
think there was never less than
ten people that made their home
there, the family and others. As
I remember, there were ten
double beds besides the two or
three couches that could be used
in an emergency.[34]

Full view of Floral

B—21

Quilt: HEXAGON

Category: Pieced

Size: 80¾" x 60"

Date: 1869 Started (dated)
       1900 Finished

Maker: Abigail Scott Duniway
        (1834–1915)

Year Over Trail: 1852

Came: As a daughter with parents,
John Tucker and Ann Roelofson
Scott, and her three brothers and
six sisters; uncle and aunt Levi
and Martha Roelofson Caffee, and
her sons; cousin William Goudy
and family; cousin John Goudy;
five drivers and three travelers including a photographer

County Where Settled: Clackamas
County, Linn County, then
Multnomah County, Oregon

Detail of typewritten documentation on quilt

In recent studies of quilt history,
this silk hexagon quilt has come to
symbolize the use of patchwork by
enlightened nineteenth-century
women. Acknowledged as not being
artistically beautiful or exceptionally
well crafted, it is now widely exhibited and written about as the work
of Abigail Scott Duniway, business
woman, journalist, and one of the
premier women's suffrage leaders in
the country.

The quilt was begun in 1869 after
her son Ralph's birth and finished in
1900. Typewritten on an orange ribbon centered in the border of the
quilt is the following documentation:

> This quilt was pieced in Novem-
> ber 1869 by Abigail Scott
> Duniway of Oregon and was
> finished and quilted by her in
> November 1900, and donated to
> the First National Woman Suf-
> frage Bazaar in honor of
> Theodore Roosevelt, the first
> champion of the equal Suffrage
> movement ever elected to a Na-
> tional office by popular vote.[35]

The plaid and plain silk two-and-
one-quarter-inch hexagons were cut
from the materials she purchased for
her millinery shop in Albany, Linn
County, Oregon. The millinery shop,
which she opened in 1866, was a
respectable way for a woman of her
time to earn an income.

Immediately upon learning of the
plan to send the quilt to the 1899
New York World's Fair as an example
of the accomplishments of Oregon
women, the Portland Woman's Club
raised a special fund to purchase the
quilt for the Oregon Historical Society, claiming it was too precious
to send out of state. Abigail Scott
Duniway donated the money to the
suffrage campaign of 1900.

The attention given to this quilt is
ironic because it is well known that
Mrs. Duniway disliked sewing and,
especially, patchwork. Writing in an
editorial on quilts in her July 15,
1880, issue of the *New Northwest*
after attending the Oregon State
Fair, she stated:

> Any fool can make a quilt;
> and after we had made a couple
> of dozen over twenty years ago,
> we quit the business with a
> conviction that nobody but a

fool would spend so much time
in cutting bits of dry goods into
yet smaller bits and sewing them
together again, just for the sake
of making believe that they are
busy at practical work.[36]

Abigail Scott Duniway

Full view of Hexagon

Detail of fabric and piecing

Although she disliked sewing, especially frivolous handwork, she realized the successful store was a way for her to establish contact with women. She soon learned the vast range of experiences shaping their lives and used that background to focus her work for women's rights, especially the right to vote.

Abigail Scott Duniway was born the second daughter of John Tucker and Ann Roelofson Scott on October 22, 1834, in Tazewell County, Illinois. Always acknowledged as an independent spirit, her life from the very beginning was influenced by the wide range of her own experiences inflicted by personal needs and the demands of society.

Abigail was assigned by her father the task of keeping a record of their journey west with the intention of future publication. Her younger sister, Harriet, later noted:

I still can "see" her as she was, a slight young girl, evenings after the weary stretches of travel with that old book in her lap—sitting either by the tent—or perchance one of the wagon wheels—or sitting on the ground—while our father was giving her commands to lay the Diary correct!—she was too weary at times to write—But always did her best.[37]

This record was the basis for several of Abigail's publications, including her 1859 *Captain Gray's Company, or Crossing the Plains and Living in Oregon* and her 1905 *From the West to the West: Across the Plains to Oregon.* Her writings draw deeply from her personal life and involvement.

Arriving in Oregon, she taught school but soon married Benjamin Duniway in 1853 and settled at first in Clackamas County. The couple eventually had six children born between 1854 and 1869.

Abigail Scott Duniway's words and actions have become banners to rally behind in the twentieth century: "When woman's true history shall have been written, her part in the upbuilding of this nation will astound the world."[38]

B–22

Quilt: LOG CABIN

Category: Pieced

Size: 54" x 36"

Date: 1875–1900

Maker: Grace Jane Simpson Skeeters
(1839–1924)

Year Over Trail: 1853

Came: As a daughter with parents,
Francis and Sarah Linder McIntire
Simpson, and eight brothers and
sisters

County Where Settled: Multnomah
County, then Jackson County,
Oregon

Grace Jane Simpson Skeeters with the quilt

The nine-inch wool squares of red
and green are built around a center
of green. This is unusual because the
centers of log cabin quilts of this
period usually were either red or
yellow, a practice thought to reflect
the hearth or the light within the
log cabin.

The quilt was donated to the
Southern Oregon Historical Society
in the mid-1970s during a time
when volunteers were in charge of
the textiles. Both the teal green twill
binding and the synthetic backing
are twentieth-century materials
added to a nineteenth-century piece.
Of course, this is unacceptable by
today's standards, but the piece has
special interest because the maker
compiled a sixteen-page typewritten
autobiography. The accomplishments
achieved within her life are examples
for future generations to honor and
cherish.

Grace Jane Simpson Skeeters was
born in Nelson County, Kentucky, in
1839, the seventh child of Francis
and Sarah Simpson. In 1841 the
family moved to Adair County, Missouri. The father and second oldest
son went to the gold fields in 1849.
Francis returned in 1852 to bring
the rest of the family to Oregon to
join the son the following spring.

Coming first to Portland, Grace's
family operated a boarding house.
In 1858 they moved to southern
Oregon to Sterlingville, a mining
town near Jacksonville, where her
father started another boarding-
house.

In 1859 she married Isaac
Skeeters, a member of the Hillman
party who discovered Crater Lake in
southern Oregon. Over the years,
they lived on a number of ranches,
eventually trading the last for several
lots in the town of Medford, about
an acre of land with a large, eight-
room house. It was here that Grace
lived with her youngest daughter,
Addie.[39]

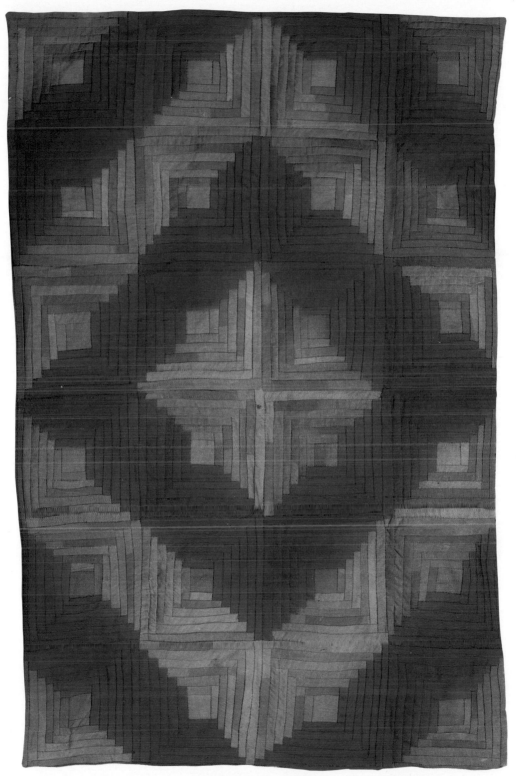

Full view of Log Cabin

B—23

Quilt: CRAZY QUILT

Size: 82" x 81½"

Date: 1894 dated

Maker: Annis Parsons Bonnett
(1814–1902)

Year Over Trail: 1854

Came: As a wife with husband,
Samuel Jasper Bonnett, and family

County Where Settled: Lane County,
Oregon

Detail with "Mrs. Annis Bonnett Age 72 1894"

The Bonnett Crazy Quilt displays two styles of construction that can be used in this type of silk quilt. The center is "uncontained," meaning the design flows freely over the surface of the quilt, while the borders are "contained," whereby geometric shapes and fans give the sense of containment and control to the design.

This style of quilt became popular after the nation's Centennial Exposition of 1876 when the public was introduced to a stunning display of Japanese art and artifacts. The peak of interest was in the mid-1880s when women's publications were still promoting the concept of the "sphere of domesticity" and the creation of a pleasant environment in which to raise a family. Publications printed how-to instructions, commentary on appropriateness, and advertisements for fabrics, kits, threads, and patterns.[40]

When compared with the many richly decorated and heavily embellished crazy quilts, this one has a special attraction. The simple marks and symbols stem-stitched on the pieces and the feather-stitched seam lines create an appropriate background for drawing attention to the central feature of the quilt, the pink ribbon with the maker's name, date, and age in black thread: "Mrs. Annis Bonnett Age 72 1894."

Crazy quilts were made to celebrate people's lives and often included fabrics from their silk clothing. Without documentation, it is impossible to validate this about this quilt, but it definitely can be said that it honors the life of a woman who came to Oregon in

1854, survived the journey, and successfully established her family.

Annis Parsons Bonnett was born in Virginia about 1814. She married Samuel Jasper Bonnett in Van Buren County, Iowa, in November 1840. They emigrated to Oregon in 1854 and became the third family to settle in Eugene in 1855. In 1857 they settled on a claim on the McKenzie River outside of Eugene. Together they raised eleven children.

Full view of Crazy Quilt

W.H.JACKSON

1856–1870

TRAIL

Becomes commercialized with trading posts, stage-coach stops, road houses, telegraph lines—no longer empty horizons and sense of loneliness as route becomes more secure.

Indians become a real challenge because of increased deaths, changes in buffalo herds, and threat to native lands.

Major problem was fear and disrespect shown the Indians by the emigrants.

Numbers going increase significantly with supplies of food and water decreasing and disease increasing.

Travel time shortened by another month.

Emigration declined during the Civil War.

QUILTS

Of the study's thirteen quilts:
  Seven were quilted when came.
  Four were quilted after.
  One pieced on the Trail.
  One made while waiting in Ohio.
Span of time represented by quilts circa 1850–1880
Number by year (family)
  1856: 0
  1857: 0
  1858: 0
  1859: 0
  1860: 1 (1)
  1861: 0
  1862: 0
  1863: 2 (2)
  1864: 7 (5)
  1865: 2 (2)
  1866: 0
  1867: 0
  1868: 1 (1)
  1869: 0
  1870: 0
Unknown: 1
Categories of quilts:
  Appliquéd: Four
  Pieced: Nine

Themes:
  Migration: Four
  Celebration: Four

QUILT MAKERS

Age range from 9 to 55.
Five came with husbands.
Three came with parents.
Two came as widow with adult children.
One came with extended family.
One making first migration.
Four making second migration.
One making third migration.

None died on the Trail.

Reasons for coming:
  Three came for economic and business opportunities.
  Three came for religious opportunities.
  Two came for land.
  Two came because against slavery.
  Two came to improve living conditions.
Number of husbands going to gold fields:
  Two went before coming to Oregon.
Four settled in Washington Territory
Four settled in the Willamette Valley:
  Two in Yamhill County
  One each in Clackamas and Lane
Two in Jackson County in southern Oregon.
One in Umatilla County in eastern Oregon.
Moved again after arriving in Oregon:
  Two to Umatilla County in northeastern Oregon
  One to Washington Territory
Role achieved in Oregon:
  Seven worked to establish homes and families.
  Two participated in communal society work.
  Two unknown.

QUILTING ACTIVITY

Before:
  Five quilted between zero and five years of coming.
  One quilted between five and fifteen years.
  One quilted between fifteen and twenty-five years.
  Four unknown.
After:
  One quilted between zero and five years of arriving.
  Four quilted between five and fifteen years.

The Trail

AFTER CROSSING THE CONTINENTAL DIVIDE near South Pass City, the Trail continued toward the West. At this time exhaustion, starvation, and the rugged terrain ahead were the main challenges. Food and water supplies for the company were diminished just when it was necessary to muster as much strength as possible to cross the rivers and mountains ahead. These depleted resources were often the deciding factor in choosing the route to follow during the last third of the journey.

As they traveled toward the most challenging and difficult part of the Trail, the trains came to the dividing points for other trails and routes, requiring the pioneers to make decisions for which there was often no return. Information posted or passed by word of mouth would give the latest knowledge about the route conditions ahead. Sometimes it was accurate and up to date, but other times it was not.

As the years of the Trail experience continued, new and better routes were always under consideration. Almost from the beginning in 1843, alternate routes were sought to avoid the difficult crossing of the Blue Mountains and the challenging float by canoe and raft down the Columbia River toward the primary destination of Oregon City, the territorial capital. The river trip from the Methodist Mission at Wascopum (The Dalles) was a costly and dangerous negotiation through the narrowest part of the river and over some of the largest falls. Often the conditions on land were as dangerous. There were delays while people waited for opportunities to get on the river. The supplies would become scarce, and the prices would be high.

The difficulty experienced by Lavina Elizabeth Frazier Wright's family (Quilt A−11) as they rafted down the Columbia River was due to severe wind and rain that prevented them from being able to land. Finally after landing and unloading, William McHaley found a fresh cow hide which he singed over the fire to remove the hair and from which he made soup. Although it resembled glue in appearance, no one refused to eat it.

Two of the most popular route options became the Applegate Trail and the Barlow Road.

Applegate Trail

As early as 1846, Jesse Applegate and others sought to find a southern route to Oregon by leaving the main trail and following the Humbolt River. His was the first wagon train, which included Elizabeth Currier Foster's party, to try this proposed route. The group turned south on the California road at Fort Hall, heading west until they got to the place where Reno is today, then turning north toward Oregon. They laid over for sixteen days in the area of High Rock Canyon while the men of the train worked to clear the route over the Calapooia Mountains. It was during this time that Elizabeth had to ride horseback and help drive the cattle. She and her sister were the first white women through the Cow Creek Canyon of southern Oregon.[1]

On the Applegate Trail in the southern Cascades, George W. Riddle, pioneer of 1851, described the crossing as the worst ten miles he had been through since leaving the Missouri River. He told of having to brace the wagons against trees by blocking them with ropes and pulleys to prevent them from overtaking the teams or overturning or sliding. Then, once on the valley floor, the walls of the canyon would be right down to the water's edge, requiring the wagons to be driven through creeks often blocked by fallen logs and boulders. It was a slow and strenuous ordeal coming near the end of the long, exhausting journey.[2]

In spite of the challenges, the Applegate Trail became popular and was used as the fastest route to southern Oregon and the lower end of the Willamette Valley.

Crossing the Blue Mountains

Those who remained on the Oregon Trail after crossing the Snake River and Grande Ronde Valley came to the first set of difficult mountains to cross, the Blue Mountains in eastern Oregon, named by David Thompson in 1811 because of their azure hue. They were not as spectacular and scenic as the Cascades, which were farther on, but they were more difficult to traverse because of the continuous series of ridges with deep draws broken by few good passes.[3]

Coming out of these mountains, the pioneers then faced the sandy soils of the high desert areas of eastern Oregon. The burden would be to move the wagons through the soft ground as they sank under the weight of household goods and people. It was here in 1852 that Lucinda Powell Propst (Quilt B–12) was buried at Butter Creek, a popular location for rest and regrouping.

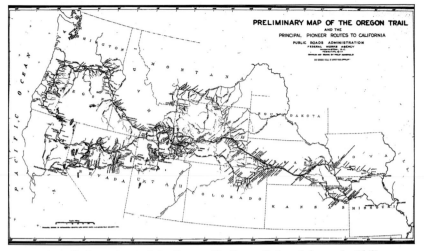

A preliminary map of the Oregon Trail compiled and drawn by Philip Mansfield

Nearing the Columbia River and The Dalles required another decision on possible routes, the river trip or the overland trip. In the steep mountains of the northern Cascades, near Mount Hood and Laurel Hill, there were rapidly flowing streams and boulder-filled gulches. The constant autumn rains challenged all who traveled. The crossing became all the more difficult for women carrying babies and toddlers. While the women walked, the men lowered the wagons using log chains and ropes to keep them under control.

Barlow Toll Road

As an alternative, in 1846 Sam Barlow was granted a license by the provisional legislature to construct a toll road east from Philip Foster's place in rural Clackamas County. By the fall of 1848, the two men, working in partnership, had cut through thickets and over streams on the south side of Mount Hood to create an eighty-mile road passable in its entire length by wagon train. Between 1846 and 1849 a total of 1,150 wagons with 5,770 people came in over the Barlow Road to Foster's place where many rested and camped until moving out into other areas of the Willamette Valley.[4] This road had a major impact on the journey of many emigrants. Diaries and journals refer to Phil Foster's place as a sign of having successfully completed the trail. It was a supply base, a meeting place, and a camp location.

The Treasures Used on the Trail

While some quilts were packed as treasures in the trunks, to be brought out and caressed once the Trail journey was complete, others were kept at hand for immediate use: as bedding, as protection, as decorative items, as shared interaction with other women, and as part of family-life rituals. Thus, their primary function was to offer moments of peace, security, and cultural identity when their owners were faced with exhaustion, isolation, illness, and death in the vast realm of the unknown through which they were traveling.

Quilts as Bedding

The primary use of quilts on the Trail was as bedding. They were used on the beds installed in the wagons, in the tents set up each night for camping, and in the bed rolls for those sleeping on the ground. A good night of rest in a comfortable and secure place was important to the success of the journey.

In 1852 two young brothers, James M. Cornwell, age seventeen, and Francis M., age nineteen, started from Iowa on foot for the Pacific Coast with a total of five dollars between them. They signed on as teamsters for emigrants in exchange for food and wagon space for their small bundles of clothing. After reaching Fort Boise, they were told by the leaders that because of short rations, it would be best for them to go on ahead with a party of six other men for possible better luck. Crossing the Alkali Flats and the John Day River, members of the starved group gradually dropped off until only the two brothers were left. Exhausted, starving, and almost delirious, the Cornell brothers finally came upon the sheltered camp of a family. Short on food themselves, they provided each with a quilt and allowed them to sleep in the wagon. Recovered the next morning, the brothers pushed on to The Dalles and eventually the Willamette Valley.[5]

It was frequently specifically suggested that each traveler bring two or three blankets or comforters (quilts), which indicates the importance of having enough of them for the trip. Once pioneers arrived, they also would need them while establishing a home.[6]

Quilts as Protection Against the Elements of Weather

Quilts were used to line or insulate the walls of the wagons against weather, wind, and Indian attacks. Nathaniel Myer, at age sixty-six, described the March days of his family's journey from Iowa's Des Moines River Valley to the southern Oregon Rogue River Valley in 1853:

> M. 25th.—Clear at s.r., white frost. The women all engaged airing the bed and other cloth which they much need. The rain and storm wetted a good many of them the two previous nights and one day.[7]

Another traveler, Andrew McClure, wrote in his journal:

> June 22nd . . . The morning cold and unpleasant. Overcoats, gloves, and comforts (quilts) again came into active use, and even then it was a bitter task to stand the blast.[8]

Quilts Used to Relieve Homesickness and Loneliness

Quilts and carpets were also used as decorative items in the tents and wagons to help relieve homesickness and sadness caused by leaving friends and relatives behind and to create a homelike setting. In addition, they served as privacy barriers to wall off sleeping and dressing areas in the tents, much as they were used in the one-room cabin homes.

Quilts as Shared Cultural Identity

Women shared their lives by exchanging recipes, needlework and quilt patterns, and fabrics from their piecing bags, all extensions of the practices and routines of their life back home. Charlotte Stearns Pengra noted in her diary in June 1853 after she entertained a visit from a woman in another wagon: "[Mrs. Smith] woshes the pattern of my sunbonnet, which I gave her with pleasure."[9]

Quilts Used in Death and Burial

Quilts used as burial shrouds were fairly common. Because of the deterioration of the water supply and an increase in the number of people traveling the Trail in close proximity, there was an epidemic of illness and disease often resulting in death.

Since wood was scarce for coffins, families used what was available and appropriate, both in size and meaning. Wrapping someone in a quilt was a way of preparing the body for burial, but it also gave reassurance to the living that the deceased person was still linked to his or her family. The Robbins family (Quilt B–11) buried their three nieces, victims of the cholera epidemic of 1852, along the Platte River after placing them together on a mattress in a wagon box covered with quilts and blankets.

Quilts as Commodities

Quilts had monetary value. In diaries and records of trail activities, they are listed as items used to trade. John Boardman noted in 1843 on the Columbia River:

> Sunday, October 15th . . . We then determined to sell our animals at the Fort and go down the river in canoes. Sold our mules for $12 each, and horses for $10. Bought a canoe for 1 blanket and 2 shirts; traded it for a larger one and gave a blanket &c to boot, and got things ready to go.[10]

Quilts were used as toll payment for the Barlow Toll Road on Mount Hood in Oregon. The following listing is a record of the Barlow-Rector-Palmer Wagon Train, showing the drivers and number of wagons and how much was paid, both in coin and in kind. The record was found in the Philip Foster Papers. One quilt was taken as equivalent to five dollars, the cost for one wagon to use the toll road.

A SAMPLE OF THE 1848 WAGON TRAIN TOLL PAYMENTS

Sept. 15				
Peter Hibbard	3 wagon-14# Powder		$7.95	Paid
C. P. Chatman	1 " -1 blanket		2.50	"
Hen Henningen	1 "	5.00 Due	4.95	"
Buford Smith	2 "	very sick		
Thomas Donca	1 "	Pd. Coat, pants, and shirt		
John Lane	1 "	Ran like a Turkey		
George Irwin	1 "	5.00 Due	5.00	Paid
W. Aceotty	10 horses	Order on McKinley		
Sept. 20, 1848				
H. V. Holmes	2 wagons	10.00 Due	10.00	Paid
J. H. Lewis	1 "	Paid 2 shirts		
Ira A. Hooker	4 "	20.00 Due	19.95	Paid
Isaac Ball	1 "	5.00 Due	5.00	Paid
Wm Porter	1 "	Paid 1 quilt		
Stephen Porter	1 "	" "		
W. L. Adams	1 "	" " "		
J. M. Blackaby	1 "	" " "	1.50	Paid
Sam Tucker	2 "	" " Bedspread	5.00	"[11]

Quilts Made on the Journey

As women came prepared to do their sewing on the trip, it was natural that they turned to piecing and appliquéing while on the slow-moving wagons or when sharing the time of rest in the evening.

Quilts included in this study that were made on the Trail seem to show that their makers were responding to the environment in choosing their designs and techniques. Sarah Koontz Glover (Quilts A–12 and A–13) pieced the small scraps of fabric for her Pinwheel and the diamond segments for her Wheel while crossing the plains in 1849. The Pinwheel reflects her response to the wind, a dramatic element of weather on the plains, especially when traveling in a cloth-covered wagon or sleeping in a fragile tent. The Wheel indicates the importance the wagon wheel played in the lives of the travelers, for if it broke they were stranded.

Isabella Fleming Mills (Quilt C–5) did the white-on-white appliqué blocks during her journey in 1865. The appliqué patterns are traditional cut-paper designs. These are examples of women using their needles and available resources to make the blocks.

Back of quilt

C–1

Quilt: SUNFLOWER

Category: Pieced

Size: 101″ x 85″

Date: circa 1860

Year Over Trail: 1863

Maker: Matilda Knight Stauffer
(1835–1867)

Came: As a daughter with her father,
Joseph; stepmother, Catharine;
and all his family, which included
sons Adam, Joseph, William, and
George (no mention of daughters'
names)[12]

County Where Settled: Willapa Bay,
Washington Territory

This handmade quilt of bright
primary colors is the frequent choice
of Pennsylvania German quiltmakers.
The detailed piecing of the quilt's
thirty-two diamond segments for
each of the twenty blocks and the
double rows of quilting indicate the
vast amount of work involved in
producing this unusual quilt. There
is extensive quilting in the unbroken
plume that moves around the border
in a meandering curve. A hex wheel
pattern is interspersed along the
border at the curve of the plume.

The back of the quilt is as interesting as the front. It contains large
strips of various plaid fabrics. This
indicates the amount of time the
young single woman had to devote
to quilt construction, and it may
also be an example of the shared
effort that existed within the Bethel–
Aurora Communal Society because
others were available to help.

The Joseph and Sarah Gates
Knight family had joined the Bethel
Colony after being approached by
Dr. William Keil in Pennsylvania.
Prior to Sarah's death in 1843, they
moved to Shelby County, Missouri,
home of the Bethel Colony. Around
1845 the family moved to Bethel
where Joseph married Catharine
Bauer, a widow with five children;
and they "conduced to the Bethel
Fund the following in money and
valuables $53.00."[13]

After Joseph Knight's two-year
stay (1853–1855) in the Northwest
as one of Dr. Keil's ten scouts
chosen to select a new location for
the colony, he returned to Bethel.
The family came with the second
Bethel–Aurora wagon train in 1863.
Although Dr. Keil had rejected the
Willapa site in Washington Territory,
choosing instead the Aurora site
south of Portland, the Knight family
went to Willapa.

There, sometime between 1863
and 1867, Matilda Knight married
Jacob Stauffer. She died giving birth
to twins in 1867. She and one baby
were buried on the farm and later
were moved to the Menlo, Washington, cemetery. The other twin,
Matilda Stauffer, was raised by
Jacob's sisters at the family home.
The quilt has passed through her
family to be treasured now by her
great-granddaughter, Vera Kocher
Yoder.[14]

Matilda Knight Stauffer

Full view of Sunflower

DRIFTWOOD LIBRARY
OF LINCOLN CITY
801 S.W. Highway 101
Lincoln City, Oregon 97367

C–2

Quilt: HONEYSUCKLE

Category: Appliqué

Size: 94″ x 80″

Date: circa 1850

Maker: Great-great-aunts of Minnie Robison Colver (1880–1960)

Year Over Trail: 1864 or 1853

Sent: With either Blin Carlos and Demaris McClain Goddard and family in 1864 or Robert Boyd and Susan Milligan Robison and family in 1853

County Where Settled: Jackson County, Oregon

This red and green quilt is composed of nine twenty-two-inch blocks with the wheel motif in the quilting design featuring a double circle with double lines across the center. Wheels appear scattered over the surface, along with hearts, flowers, and wreaths in much the same format as other quilts with wheels. These expressions of affection are most often identified with wedding quilts. It is likely that this wheel represents migration and the blessing of good wishes associated with leave-taking.

A rather unusual feature is the vine border appearing on three sides, with the vacant edge being one of the long sides. Usually the vacant edge is either the top or the bottom, indicating it would be covered by pillows or used on a bed with a foot. Quilts with definite border construction patterns often indicate having been made for specific beds. In this case, it would be one in which the long side was against a wall or it was a bed with a wooden sideboard to be displayed, thus no need to show a quilt border.

Detail of "wheels" in quilting

The Honeysuckle appliqué design is another unique feature. According to Elly Sienkiewicz, the nineteenth-century meaning of the honeysuckle was "devotion, generous affection, mirth, love's bond, and 'we belong to one another.'"[15]

The quilt was made by the great-great-aunts of the donor, Minnie Robison Colver. They would have been the sisters of either Blin Carlos Goddard (1822–1893) or John Francis Robison (1799–1870). Blin Carlos Goddard was born in New York and migrated West in 1837 to Missouri. His wife, Demaris Mc-Clain (1826–1893), was born in North Carolina and moved with her family to Missouri in 1835. The Goddard couple were married in

1844 and came over the Oregon Trail in 1864. Both John Robison and his wife, Susan Milligan (1806–1889), were born in Pennsylvania. They married in 1822 in Ohio, moved to Iowa in 1847, and came to Oregon in 1853.

Both Goddard and Robison had sisters whose lifespans would coincide with making a quilt in the 1840s for their brothers. The quilt could very well have been a migration and/or wedding quilt made for either couple.[16]

Full view of Honeysuckle

C-3

Quilt: PRINCESS FEATHER

Category: Appliqué

Size: 88″ x 64″

Date: circa 1860

Maker: Margaret Fuson Lieuallen
(1838–1931)

Year Over Trail: 1864

Came: As a wife with husband,
William T., and his brother

County Where Settled: Umatilla
County, Oregon

The red and green appliqué continued to be popular for this period of time and place. This quilt is less elaborate than many of the earlier ones that often included intricate borders and quilting designs. Here the work is straightforward and practical: five large appliqué blocks of thirty-four inches arranged with one cut in half and placed at one end to give needed additional length. This is an unusual set.

The quilting designs are simple and practical. In and between the feathers are short chains of diamonds. The rest is a gridwork of diagonal and straight lines placed about one-half inch apart.

According to the family history, the quilt may have been made by Margaret Lieuallen and her mother, Sarah Moody Fuson, prior to the younger woman's marriage and migration.

Beneath the tree by the spring just a year ago Margaret had promised William Lieuallen to

William Lieuallen, Margaret Fuson Lieuallen, and baby Johnny; sons Thomas and James standing.

leave her home in Kentucky and travel by covered wagon to make her home in far away Oregon. This afternoon in a simple ceremony she would become his wife and tomorrow they were joining a caravan bound for Oregon. The wagon was carefully loaded, the oxen fat and well broken.

How fast the year had passed, now so soon the dear ones would be left behind. Mother and daughter had worked long hours together, the quilts so painstakingly pieced and quilted, the heavy wool filled comforters, the homespun dresses, the simple household linens now all packed and loaded ready for the long journey.[17]

Coming later to Oregon in 1864, the Lieuallens elected to settle in northeastern Oregon in the Pine Creek area of the Blue Mountains in Umatilla County. William chose to claim this rugged, isolated, and exposed land because of a spring of water and the open range pasture for his cattle.

Full view of Princess Feather

Detail of star and triangle piecing

C–4

Quilt: STARS WITH WILD
   GEESE STRIPS

Category: Pieced

Size: 82" x 60"

Date: circa 1880

Maker: Margaret Fuson Lieuallen
   (1838–1931)

Year Over Trail: 1864

Came: As a wife with husband,
   William T., and his brother and
   his family

County Where Settled: Umatilla
   County, Oregon

This pieced quilt reflects the migration theme in its sense of movement and convergence created by the diamonds and triangles. Although the name given to the pattern by the family was not recorded, a similar pattern found in Missouri at the same time was called Railroad and Depot.[18] Another name is the Spider Web, a tribute to the effort a spider exerts to create a place in time and space.[19]

Studying the quilt provides clues that date it later than the Lieuallen migration: the Centennial fabric in one star which reads "1776–1876" and the color fastness of the bright pink as compared to the other fabrics of the quilt.[20] Many of the print fabrics used in the triangles and diamonds span the years before and after the maker's 1864 marriage and migration.

Margaret and William Lieuallen had three sons born between 1865 and 1871. The youngest died at the age of six in 1877. After William Lieuallen suffered seizures, much of the work on their ranch was done by his wife.

Margaret kept a cow for milk and chickens for eggs. She planted a garden every spring and had a cellar behind the house for storage of vegetables, canned fruits, and pans of milk. William had planted an extensive orchard with apple, cherry, pear, walnut, and persimmon trees,

and grape vineyards. He loved to offer a persimmon before it was ripe and watch the reaction to the bitter and puckery taste.

Grandma Lieuallen smoked a pipe, and Aunt Sarah Lieuallen used snuff, but they thought any woman who smoked a cigarette was, in their words, "a hussy." Grandma had started smoking because of a digestive problem.[21]

Full view of Stars with Wild Geese Strips

C–5

Quilt: WILD GOOSE CHASE
  VARIATION

Category: Pieced

Size: 84" x 61"

Date: circa 1865–1880

Maker: Sarah Moody Fuson
  (?–1898)

Year Over Trail: Late—perhaps by
  railroad

Came: Unknown

County Where Settled: Umatilla
  County, Oregon

Detail of fabric and quilting

This handmade quilt was made by Sarah Moody Fuson, mother of Margaret Lieuallen, while she was in Missouri. It has the migration theme of movement and change in its strip piecing of triangles. The quilt shows some wear, particularly in the fading from pink to white of the triangles near the center of each block. The elbow/fan quilting is again reflective of the period in terms of purpose, making bed covers within a reasonable length of time for regular use. This style of quilt is also known to have been a product of a group effort.

The borders are interesting to speculate about since the brown ones on three sides vary in size. The treatment is similar to Quilt C–2, with no border on one long side. Perhaps it was for a bed against a wall; perhaps the maker used the fabric she had and ignored the fourth side. The second border matches the fabric of the backing.

There was a strong bond between mother and daughter. According to the family history, Margaret Lieuallen was reluctant to leave her mother, Sarah Fuson, in Missouri at the time of her 1864 marriage and migration. Sarah's response was that she would never leave her father who had provided a home for her and her three children when they needed it. Her husband, James Fuson, had died in Knox County, Kentucky, prior to the move to Missouri. There were several sons, but no actual record of them exists.

A family history note indicates that while Sarah Fuson Moody was still living in Missouri, and to prevent her being put in the poorhouse, William Lieuallen planned to bring her to his home. However, she was put on the train (railroad or wagon?) and came alone. She died in 1898 while living with Margaret and William Lieuallen in northeastern Oregon. At her death, a special coffin had to be made because she was so stooped.[22]

Full view of Wild Goose Chase Variation

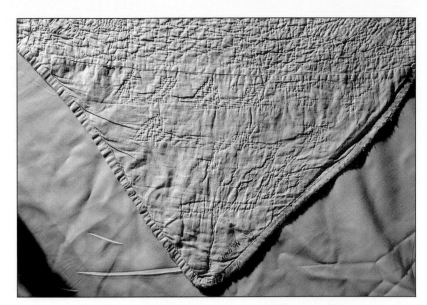

Detail with "Bell Mills born Aug 11, 1835" in quilting

C–6

Quilt: WHITE ON WHITE

Category: Appliqué

Size: 72″ x 66″

Date: 1863 Started
   Finished later

Maker: Isabella Fleming Mills
   (1835–1907)

Year Over Trail: 1863

Came: As a wife with husband,
   George W. Mills, and their six
   children

County Where Settled: Yamhill
   County, Oregon, then Thurston
   County, Washington Territory

This quilt is difficult to see and
study, but it is important as an
example of a project started while on
the Trail. However, the study of a
white-on-white quilt that has been
used and laundered is often reward-
ing. Because the family history states
the quilt was made while crossing
the plains in 1863, a commitment
was made to examine and photograph the quilt. George Champlin
of the Oregon Historical Society
tried to solve the photographic challenge within budget and resources.

Being made on the Trail refers to
the appliqué work done on the
individual blocks. The blocks are
nine cut-paper designs drawn on
white cloth and hand appliquéd on
sixteen-inch squares of white. The
set of blocks is on point, where the
blocks are joined at the corners
rather than at the edges. This more
difficult arrangement, as well as the
extensive amount and intricacy of
quilting, indicates it was quilted after
the family arrived in the Northwest
when the quilt could have been
placed on a large flat surface and in
a quilt frame.

The quilting lines reveal four different large wheel patterns quilted
over the surface. Hearts, flowers, and

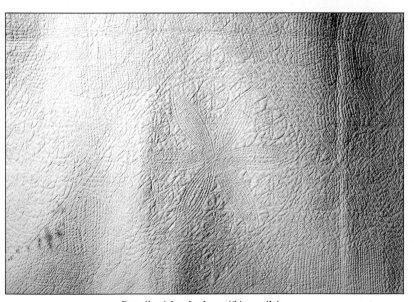

Detail with wheel motif in quilting

wheels are scattered randomly over
the quilt top. There appears to be a
pair of open scissors in the corner of
one block; in another corner is the
maker's notation: "Bell Mills born
Aug 11th, 1835."

Isabelle Fleming and George W.
Mills were married in Illinois in
1853. They migrated to Missouri

where he fought in the Civil War at
Kirksville. A war injury, along with
the "bitter hard times" in Missouri
and the cry of gold in California,
precipitated the couple's decision to
migrate West. At the Platte River,
the military advised them to arrange
to go with other wagons for safety.
The train they joined was destined

Full view of White on White

for Oregon instead of California, so
the Mills changed their plans. They
were grateful for the advice when
they came upon several scenes of
disastrous raids.

Arriving in Oregon, they settled
in Yamhill County where their son
George was born. In 1865 they
moved to Thurston County, Washington Territory, after receiving
encouraging letters from former
neighbors. When she saw the salt
water before her, Mrs. Mills is re-
ported to have said, "Well, Pa, this is
the jumping off place. We haven't
the money to go back; we can go no
further, so we've just got to stay
here."[23] Eventually they settled in
the South Union area six miles from
Tumwater.

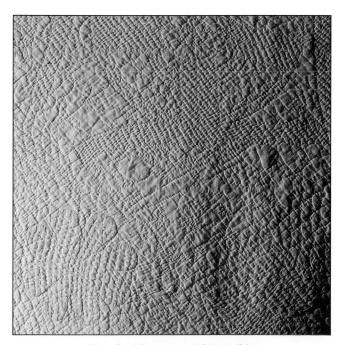

Detail with scissor motif in quilting

C–7

Quilt: BASKET

Category: Pieced

Size: 74″ x 68″

Date: circa 1860s

Maker: Nancy Callaway Nye (1810–1883)

Year Over Trail: 1865

Came: As an older woman but unclear who brought her

County Where Settled: Clark County, Washington Territory, Umatilla County, Oregon

Detail of fabric fading

This pieced quilt of empty baskets is made with a predominance of four fabrics, which indicates that fabric in quantities was available to the quilter. The backing fabric matches the solid-block fabric on the front. This fabric has faded from gray to tan, although it may have started as a purple. It is unusual and perhaps is an example of why gray fabric does not appear often in quilts of this period.[24]

A note reading "Grandma Nancy's quilt, brought from Missouri" was attached to the quilt when it was found among her granddaughter's personal belongings after her death.

Nancy Callaway Nye is typical of the women in the study who came West as widows accompanying or joining their children. The idea of staying behind when one's children "took leave" was difficult to accept and often encouraged a widowed mother, a maiden aunt, or a cousin to join the migration.

Nancy was born in 1810 in Ashe County, North Carolina, the daughter of Thomas Callaway and Elizabeth Ray Callaway. In 1826, the family moved to Wythe County, Virginia, where Nancy married Dr. James Madison Nye on August 26, 1826. They had twelve children over

twenty-two years between 1826 and 1848. In 1840 or 1841 the family moved to Boone County in central Missouri, along the Missouri River.

In 1850 Dr. Nye and his son William started for the gold fields. Near Little Blue River, Nebraska, Dr. Nye died of cholera while trying to save the lives of others. William became ill but recovered enough to return home where he died within a year.

Gradually, as the other children grew, they migrated to the West; so by the end of the Civil War, the majority of them were living in Oregon country. In 1865 Nancy made the long trek over the Trail to Vancouver, Washington Territory, where she lived with her son John Wirt. After his early death at age thirty-five, she joined her son Ad in the Pendleton area of Umatilla County in northeastern Oregon, where she died in 1883.[25]

Nancy Callaway Nye

Full view of Basket

C–8

Quilt: BACHELOR

Category: Pieced and Appliqué

Size: 84″ x 74″

Date: 1855 Started
1869 Finished

Maker: Mary Jane Fairley Bryan
(1839–1933)

Year Over Trail: 1864

Came: As a wife with husband,
Daniel Boone Bryan, and two
children

County Where Settled: Yamhill
County, Oregon

Detail of fabric and quilting

The nine-and-one-half-inch pieced circles are made up of nine segments: four red, four green, and one orange. According to family history, the pattern is named Bachelor because the orange unit stands out in the circle; unlike the red and green pairs, the bachelor does not have a mate.[26] Probably an original name for the pattern, it fits in with the idea of a young woman making a quilt top for her hope chest, a long-established quilt tradition. The top was pieced and appliquéd by the maker while living in Guernsey County, Ohio, in 1855.

Another name for the pattern is Whirlwind, a migration theme with its meaning of movement.[27]

Feathered wreaths surround each circle with sprigs of leaves, curlicues, and grid work as fillers. Four-inch pieced strips repeat the colors in a zig-zag fashion for the border treat-

Mary Jane Fairley Bryan

ment. The binding is a black ground with green and yellow. The quilt is dated "May 25, 1869 quilted."

A handwritten note in the documentation file states that in 1858 Mary Jane Fairley married Daniel Boone Bryan and they moved from Ohio to Kentucky and then to Missouri. Crossing the Plains in 1864, they settled in Yamhill County. Eventually they had five children.[28]

Full view of Bachelor

C–9

Quilt: EIGHT-POINTED STAR

Category: Pieced

Size: 83″ x 61″

Date: circa 1873

Maker: Ersula Goddard Robison Dean (1856–1934)

Year Over Trail: 1864

Came: As a daughter with her parents, Blin Carlos and Demaris McClain Goddard, and her brothers and sisters

County Where Settled: Jackson County, Oregon

(Left to right) Willis J. Dean, Minnie Robison Colver, and Ersula Goddard Robison Dean

The fabrics of the twelve-inch hand-pieced blocks appear to be older than the date of 1873 given for construction. They may be of the mid-nineteenth century, in the colors of brown, butterscotch, and green. The quilting designs are wreaths with clam shells.

The common practice of piecing first, then quilting and completing the quilt later, would coincide with the Goddard family history. The accession record indicates that Ersula Goddard was seventeen when the quilt was made in 1873, the year before her first marriage.

She was born in 1856 in Missouri and came to Oregon in 1864 with her family. She married Robert B. Robison, and their first child was born in 1875. Robert died in 1880, and she married Willis J. Dean in 1886.[29]

It is unclear where or when the pattern name Eight-pointed Star was attached to the quilt. This particular pattern has a history of different names, showing the change with migration of pattern designs and names. It is also called Rolling Star, Brunswick Star, and Chained Star by Ruth Finley who describes it as a diamond pattern.[30]

This quilt and the Colver Quilt (C–2) are from the same family and donor, Minnie Robison Colver. The two quilts illustrate the effort made by the descendants to preserve their family history. They are providing a secure future for the quilts by donating them to a well-equipped museum, the Southern Oregon Historical Society. These quilts are important as examples of the continued interest in and need for making bed quilts throughout the nineteenth century.

A wonderful photograph exists showing the maker sitting straight in her lawn chair in front of her home in Talent, Oregon, in the 1890s. The flowering plants by the side of the house show the pride she had in her home. The planted garden in the foreground and the logged slope in the background show the fruits of the labors of Ersula and her second husband, Willis J. Dean. He was a school teacher who wrote and gave funeral addresses for people of the community. The young woman in the photograph is her daughter, Minnie Robison Colver.

Full view of Eight-pointed Star

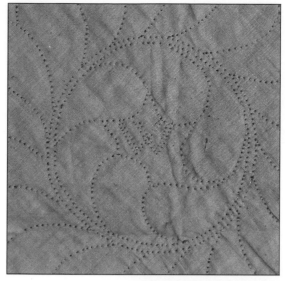

Detail of "W" in the quilting

C–10

Quilt: PINK AND GREEN

Category: Pieced

Size: 87" x 71"

Date: circa 1875

Maker: Women of Aurora Colony

Year Over Trail: Possibly 1863

Came: As members of the Bethel-Aurora Communal Society

County Where Settled: Marion County, Oregon

This pink and green pieced quilt is one of at least six that exist in Oregon and are connected with the Aurora Colony communal society. The colors and pattern are representative of quilts made by a group of German religious idealists, former members of George Rapp's Harmony–Economy who were drawn together in the late 1830s in western Pennsylvania. They approached the personable leader, Dr. William Keil, about heading an experiment in communal living, and he led the group to Bethel, Missouri, in 1844.

Successful in Missouri but eager to keep his group together and inspired by the dream of owning western land, Dr. Keil brought the group to Oregon in four wagon train migrations between 1855 and 1867. Some six hundred members of the group made their homes in Aurora and Willapa, and the colony was active until Dr. Keil's death in 1877, when its assets were divided among the members.

The colony was a special part of the history of Oregon, becoming known for its music, food, hospitality, furniture, and clothing. Credit is given to Keil, a trained tailor, for establishing a style of dress appropriate for the pioneer. Under Keil's direct influence, the women of the commune became especially skilled

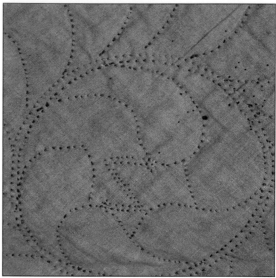

Detail of "S" in the quilting

in weaving, sewing, and embroidering.[31]

The quilt reflects the colonists' desire to share their patterns, their work, and their supplies. The color combination was a favorite with many quilters, including Germans, everywhere at the time. But this eight-and-one-half-inch pieced pattern block is common. There is no record of the pattern name used by the commune women but Crosses and Losses and Fox and Geese are

two popular ones. Wreaths quilted in the solid blocks are referred to as the "Aurora wreath."[32]

Subtly and carefully quilted within the wreaths are the letters S and W, perhaps a simple identification mark. There were families by the names of Stauffer and Wolfer in the colony.

A continuous feather plume surrounds the quilt in the seven-and-one-fourth-inch border, another common feature in the colony quilts.

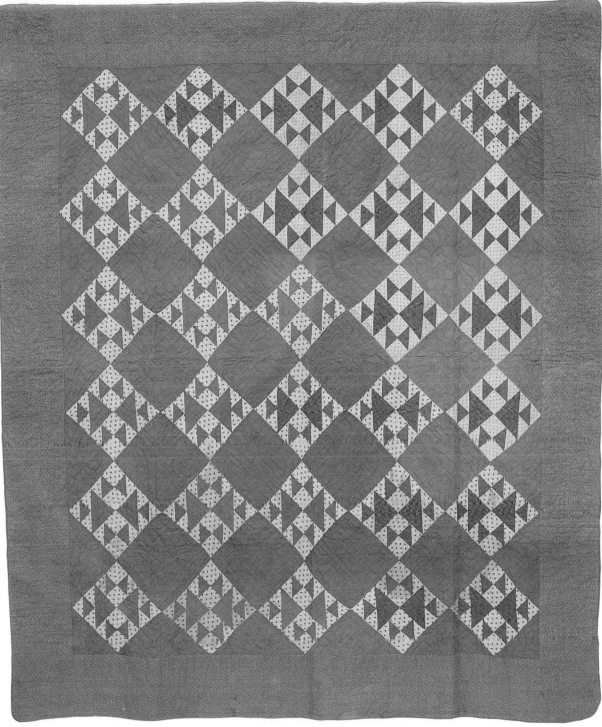

Full view of Pink and Green

PART FOUR
=
Those Who Wait

THE MAIN FOCUS OF THIS BOOK HAS BEEN the quilted treasures of the makers and their families who actually experienced the Oregon Trail. These quilts have been made before, during, or after a journey across the plains. During the search an additional component became apparent: the quilts made in the "States" during the wait for someone who went over the Trail. In this unexpected find, the grouping is small, but it is likely that as the years of celebration unfold and individual families review their family history, additional "while waiting" treasures will surface.

Nevertheless, featured here are two quilts made by young Ohio women who represent many women of the mid-nineteenth century. One quilt was a wedding gift for a brother; the other was part of a personal hope chest. They demonstrate the extensive amount of time and effort single women were able to devote to their needlework. Both communicate the romantic and supportive sentiments women of the period were encouraged to include in their quilts.

D–1

Quilt: FRUIT AND FLOWERS QUILT

Category: Appliqué

Size: 89″ x 89″

Date: circa 1855

Maker: Mary Carpenter Pickering Bell (1831–1900)

Where Made: Belmont County, Ohio

(Left to right) Seated: John Bruce Bell and Mary Carpenter Pickering Bell; standing: Bruce, Maggie, and Frank Bell.

This masterpiece quilt was made while Mary waited for the return of her friend John Bruce Bell, who had gone to Oregon from Belmont County, Ohio, in 1850. This was different than most young people of the time who would be married before crossing the Plains in order to claim more land.

The "while-waiting" quilt was found after the author read the documentation submitted by the family when it was donated to the Smithsonian Institution. The history provided by Dr. Robert Bell read:

This quilt was made by Mary Carpenter Pickering in about 1850–1854 at St. Clairsville, Belmont County, Ohio. Her friend, John Bruce Bell (1829–1912), had left St. Clairsville in 1850 to accompany a wagon train to Oregon Territory. The nineteen-year-old Mary started the quilt after his leaving "to make the time go more quickly," but he did not return until eight years later. They were married on September 3, 1861. He was shortly to join the Union Army for service in the Civil War, and while he was gone, Mary made another quilt, a "crazy" quilt which would be subjected to use. . . . John and Mary started their family in Ohio but in 1864 moved to Keokuk County, Iowa. . . . The quilt won her a

Blue Ribbon at the Ohio State Fair in the early 1850's.[1]

In the appendix is a letter written from Oregon in 1855 by Bell to Mary Carpenter Pickering. The charming letter contains much of the feeling generally expressed about the Oregon Territory. It also addresses the loneliness of being separated from friends back home.

The nine appliqué blocks contain the same basket and flowers motif. Each of the plain white blocks fea-

tures a different quilted and stuffed fruit or flower design. The unbalanced placement of the baskets suggests a less precise hand than the one that executed the intricately designed stuffwork. This leads to the supposition that the appliqué work was done earlier than the quilting and stuffwork. A family member confirmed this when she stated that her grandmother began the quilt at age thirteen.

The discrepancy on the start-date of a quilt can happen when one

Detail with "Mary C. Pickering, St. Clairsville, Ohio" embroidered

Full view of Fruit and Flowers Quilt

acknowledges possible confusion about the time it takes to make and finish a quilt, especially a masterpiece. Mary Carpenter Pickering, as suggested, probably began the appliqué work at the young age of thirteen. Then, judging from the amount of work and time required to complete an intricate quilt, it may have taken her at least four more years to finish it.

Mary Carpenter Pickering was from an affluent Quaker family in Belmont County, Ohio. She had a refined appreciation for fine linen, silver, and furniture.

Bell was a Scotch Presbyterian. A patriot loyal to the Union, he was a man of his times, eager to see the West and serve in the Civil War. In Oregon his name has been found only in the public record in an affidavit to citizenship being awarded to Edward Robson on April 9, 1855.[2]

According to family records, Mary and John were married in September 1861, M.C.D., meaning "married contrary to discipline," referring to their different religious backgrounds.[3]

D–2

Quilt: PINE TREE

Category: Pieced

Size: 80" x 76"

Date: 1849

Maker: Emma and Kate Helman

Where Made: Ashland County, Ohio

Abel and Martha Kanaga Helman and family

This turkey-red and white quilt is in the popular Pine Tree pattern. Trees have long been favorites among quiltmakers, and this variation of pieced triangles became popular in the mid-nineteenth century. The amount of effort to construct this quilt is substantial with accurate, precise piecing needed to make the design work appropriately. At the time of migration, Americans were seeking stability, and the pine tree presented the image of rootedness. The design gives an opportunity for the quilt owner to feel a sense of connectedness with friends and family separated by many miles.[4]

For one to view the trees with their strong roots upright, the set of the blocks requires the quilt to be studied from the side of the bed rather than from the head or the foot.

The accession information states the quilt was a wedding gift for Abel and Martha Kanaga Helman, married in 1849 in Ashland, Ohio, and made by the groom's sisters, Emma and Kate Helman.

Abel Helman was a man who wanted to investigate the West. "There was that urge and that surge of traveling west. There were a great many people coming west at that time, so of course he was among those who wanted to come." Married less than one year, he left his wife in Ohio, expecting just to look the situation over, then return to his hometown. Instead, he met Eber Emery in the California mines, and together they went north to southern Oregon looking for a creek location to construct a flour mill and a sawmill. Locating a likely site, they named it Ashland Creek, and then they founded a settlement named Ashland for his hometown in Ohio.[5]

In the meantime, communication between the couple was rare, and her family assumed he was not going to return. Two and one-half years later, he did return and discovered he had become a father.

In early 1853 the Helmans returned together to Ashland, Oregon, shipping their household goods around the Horn from New York City while they booked a steamer to Nicaragua, shortening their trip by almost 1,000 miles.[6]

Living in Ashland, Oregon, the Helmans led active community-oriented lives. Kanaga Helman had trained as a nurse in Ohio and had become known for her skills in doctoring illnesses and extracting teeth.[7]

It is interesting to contrast the feelings of the two Ohio families about the lives of Abel and Martha K. Helman. Her family was sure he would not return, while his family made them a Pine Tree quilt as a reminder of their roots and their connection to their Ohio home.

Full view of Pine Tree

POSTLUDE
=
After the Trail

The Arrival

THE CHALLENGING TRAIL EXPERIENCE, WHETHER merely difficult or tragic, helped to ease the families and individuals into the frontier lifestyle they would live once they reached Oregon. The Reverend George H. Atkinson noted the arrivals of emigrants in 1847:

> An immigrant will come in during the Autumn, put himself up a log house with a mud & stick chimney, split boards and shingles, break eight or ten or twenty acres of prairie and sow it with wheat. You call upon him the next year & he will have a fine field ripe for the sickle. His large field will be well fenced with newly split fir rails. There will be a patch of corn, another of potatoes, & another of garden vegetables. Outside a large piece will be broken for the present year's sowing. His cattle & horse & hogs will be on the prairie, thriving and increasing without care. A few sheep may be around the house. He has a spring near. . . . The farmer wears buckskin pants. His family has few cooking utensils, few chairs. No additions since they came into the Territory.[1]

Two Stages of Frontier Development

Reflecting on the thirty-year period over which women and their families came to the Northwest, we can see that their lives mirror those of women found in other studies of the western frontier.[2]

The first stage of establishing a home and farm took an average of two to five years. During that time, the skills developed on the Trail served the women well since they continued to live in tents and wagon boxes. Having left the East in the spring, they would arrive in Oregon around December in the early years or September in later years when travel was swifter. The first priority would be a place to winter over. This two- to five-year stage would be repeated by each group that arrived during the thirty-year span, but with differing degrees of services available.

The second stage of frontier development was the community building that evolved from the first, or survival, stage, as people began to establish social interaction with the need for resources such as churches, schools, and political and governmental units.

A. S. Duniway voting, 1914

The earliest period of Trail years (1840–1850) in Oregon was difficult for the arriving migrants since few people, houses, and services were in place. The Perkins family (Quilt A–2) noted the difficulty in finding housing during the hard winter of 1844. Elizabeth Currier Foster's family (Quilts A–3–9) was given shelter by a family in Rickerall their first year of 1846. Tabitha Moffett Brown arrived on Christmas Day at a minister's home in Salem, at the end of her long journey.*

During the second period (1851–1855), arrival and adjustment became easier for many of the migrants who had either families or friends to receive them. Before arrival, arrangements would have been made for a rental house or for accommodations within family homes.

By the end of their 1851 journey, the Robbins family (Quilt B–11) were ill and nearing starvation when they were rescued by their cousins, William and Noah Herren, and taken to a rented house in Salem for the winter. The Leonard family (Quilt B–2), of the Lost Wagon Train of 1853, were rescued by settlers of Lane County, the Harlows (Quilt A–16) being among the rescuers. The 1853 Bethel–Aurora scouts (Quilt B–15) met with Captain U. S. Grant at Fort Vancouver upon their arrival and followed his recommendation that they winter at Fort Steilacoom, a military outpost on the Puget Sound in Washington Territory, until the weather was favorable.

In the later period (1856–1870), migrants arrived to find established communities with full services available. The Simpson family, pioneers of 1853 (Quilt B–22), operated boardinghouses in Portland and later in Sterlingville in Jackson County. The four wagon trains arriving at the Aurora Colony in the 1860s found an established community ready to receive them:

Aurora women

> Aurora [was] like many other common villages of the period, with large houses lining the streets. . . . Each family appeared to have substantial food and clothing but there was no little ornamentation or luxury.
>
> There is evidently plenty of scrubbing indoors, plenty of plain cooking, plenty of everything that is absolutely necessary to support life . . . and nothing superfluous.[3]

Studies of women on the frontier conclude that most were desirous of returning to the cultural norm of being a wife, mother, and housekeeper once they became securely established.

A valuable contribution to this project in understanding the responses to the "sphere of domesticity," specifically by rural Oregon women, was the doctoral thesis by sociologist Christopher Carlson while at the University of Oregon. His research,

*An account of using her needleskills to establish herself is included in Appendix B.

which included many of the same families as those of this quilt project, concluded:

> While they were familiar with the ideology of domesticity, rural women certainly did not view their role as lying there in the creation of private retreats. Instead, they viewed themselves as partners in the farm enterprise. It appears that rural women were struggling with this new ideology emanating from the east and the urban middle class and not exactly sure how it applied to their own lives. They accepted responsibility for the home and raising children but were unwilling to let go of their productive role in the family and the sense of importance it gave them. Therefore, while familiar with the ideology of domesticity farm women expressed a view of the home as part of a work environment.[4]

Pioneer Association flyer, 1876

More and more people had arrived, settled, and become established, and as the years passed it became evident there should be some means of preserving the past and saving it for the future. One means for this was through creation of the Oregon Pioneer associations. They immediately became popular and their annual meetings were well attended. The program format included speeches and narratives of personal experiences along with social interactions and general reminiscences. These events were recorded and published in a journal, *Oregon Pioneer Association Transaction*, and often a group photo was taken.

At least one quilt was made to celebrate this group. Caroline Bayley Dorris Watts, the pioneer of 1845 kidnapped by Indians, was noted as having made a quilt composed entirely of Oregon

Pioneer reunion

Pioneer reunion

Pioneer Association badges. Unfortunately, it has not been found and was not available for this publication.[5]

A second method was through writing memoirs and publishing journals. The importance of needle skills was not forgotten. One pioneer of 1843, Berthina Owens-Adair, wrote of the early days, a passage often quoted in today's needlework books:

> I think the most unhappy period of my life was the first year spent on Clatsop, simply for the want of something to do. I had no yarn to knit, nothing to sew, not even rags to make patches. . . . One day Mrs. Parrish gave me a sack full of rags and I never received a present before nor since that I so highly appreciated as I did those rags.[6]

Berthina Owens-Adair (1840–?), a pioneer of 1843, lived on the Clatsop Plain until about 1853 during which time Mrs. Parrish, wife of the Methodist missionary The Reverend Josiah Parrish, was also there. Berthina Owens-Adair lived a successful life following an early failed marriage. She went from being an illiterate young mother at age eighteen to becoming a successful doctor at age fifty. Her fascinating and encouraging career history included being a laundress, a teacher, a seamstress, and owner of a millinery shop.[7]

The third method was through these quilts.

As these women began to reflect publicly and privately on their Oregon Trail experience with the tools they had been taught to use—needles, pens, and books—they created the treasures included here to show their lives. Their quilts and their written works are the records of their dreams and memories—disappoint-ments and trials as well as the accomplishments of their goals.

Through their treasured quilts, these women clearly demon-strated the conclusions of earlier studies of westering women by Jeffrey, Myres, and Schlissel. While staying within the roles per-mitted by society, and overcoming the hazards of migration and settlement, these women showed their determination in making a successful transition. Their names and stories await our celebration of their contributions to Oregon's history.

APPENDIXES

═══

APPENDIX A *Themes from the Treasures*

Quilt Patterns

SUMMARIZING THE INDIVIDUAL QUILTS INTO themes requires that one consider the options available and not available to mid-nineteenth century women. Each woman's life experience was unique. While many had limited formal education, most had extensive needlework skills. While most were occupied with producing bed linens and clothing needed in the home, many had time to create special quilts expressing passages of their lives. Although many women were isolated on the frontier, most eagerly shared their lives with one another whenever opportunities arose. While each person's preconceptions affected how they experienced the trip, all were exposed to the "shaping power" of the West on their environment. While quilts generally have been thought to have been made in one place and time, it now is known that many were begun in one location and carried to another for later completion.

The two themes most clearly identified with these quilts are those of migration and celebration. Migration themes reflect nature or an outdoor experience, movement or change of location, friendship, and well-being. They are expressed through interpreting objects connected to the pioneer era, such as an old fashioned flower or a log cabin. They can be graphically inscribed with actual words or symbols; they can be visually perceived through pattern

QUILT AND QUILT MAKER IDENTIFICATION CHART

Quilt Name	Maker/Family	Number	Page
Bachelor	Bryan	C–8	114
Basket	Nye	C–7	112
Birds in Flight variation	Riddle	B–8	60
Crazy Quilt	Bonnett	B–23	88
Delectable Mountains	Purdom/Leonard	B–2	48
Double Irish Chain I	Foster	A–5	16
Double Irish Chain II	Foster	A–8	22
Double Nine Patch	Sawtell	B–14	70
Eight-pointed Star	Dean	C–9	116
Flashing Minnow	Cox	A–15	33
Floral Applique	Morris	B–20	82
Flying Star	Foster	A–7	20
Fruit and Flowers	Pickering/Bell	D–1	123
Harlow Album Quilt	Harlow	A–16	34
Hexagon	Duniway	B–21	84
Honeysuckle	Colver	C–2	102
Hovering Hawks and Peonies	Gilfrey	B–16	74
Lily	Buell	A–10	24
Log Cabin	Skeeters	B–22	86
Mexican Lily	Foster	A–9	23
Oregon Rose	Robbins	B–11	64
Oregon Trail	Dibble	B–19	80
Peony with Flying Geese Border	Weaver	B–7	58
Pieced Star	Gilmour	B–18	78
Pine Tree	Helman	D–2	125
Pink and Green	Aurora Colony	C–10	118
Pin Wheel	Glover	A–12	28
Poke Stalk	Foster	A–3	13
Princess Feather	Lieuallen	C–3	104
Road to California	Drain	B–9	61
Rose of Sharon	Foster	A–6	18
Rose variation	Stone	B–10	62
Royal Presentation	Royal	B–17	76
Running Squares	Giesy	B–15	72
Setting Sun	Greer	B–3	50
Single Irish Chain	Merriman	B–6	56
Star	Foster	A–4	15
Star	Riggs	B–1	46
Stars with Wild Geese Strips	Lieuallen	C–4	106
Sunflower	Stauffer	C–1	100
Sun/Hexagon Blocks	Medley	A–14	32
Tufted White on White	Chambers	A–1	8
Tulip	Perkins	A–2	10
Tulip	Propst	B–12	66
Wandering Foot	Hargrave/Whiteaker	B–4	52
Wandering Foot	Morris	B–13	68
Wandering Foot	Patterson	B–5	54
Wheel	Glover	A–13	30
Wheel of Fortune	Wright	A–11	26
White on White	Mills	C–6	110
Wild Goose Chase variation	Fuson	C–5	108

and design; often they can be a visual appeal of support from a higher power, an appeal for divine guidance through the harrowing experience they faced crossing the plains.

Celebration themes reflect significant events or honors in people's lives. They honor weddings, births, faithful service, accomplishments, and successes. The most important celebration found in the quilts in this book is for having survived the wagon trip to Oregon and successfully established one's life and family in the new territory. This serves as visual evidence of these women's desire to return to and maintain the feminine role of domesticity associated with nineteenth-century women back in the States. Several outstanding examples include the Harlow Album quilt (A–16) and the Royal Presentation Album quilt (B–17) with people's names on individual blocks. The Harlow Quilt, made by Frances Harlow in 1898, celebrated her family by including the names of her daughters, granddaughters, and great granddaughters in Eugene, Oregon. Her block near the center carefully records that she pieced the quilt at age eighty-three.

The Royal Presentation quilt was made for Rev. J. H. B. Royal in 1868 and inscribed with the names of the children who lived along the Methodist Circuit Rider route he covered in southwest Washington Territory.

A third is the crazy quilt (B–23) with the inscription "Mrs. Annis Bonnett, age 72, 1894" proudly and boldly stitched across the ribbon on the front of the quilt. This clearly states who she was and what she accomplished in 1894 at age seventy-two.

Much of early life in America was spent outdoors—improving the land, planting and raising food and flowers, doing the tasks of washing, preparing food, preparing materials for making cloth, and making candles and soap. Using nature as a theme in quilt design was an established tradition in quiltmaking. The quilts made before or brought over the Trail or made while waiting confirm this: Chambers (A–1), Foster (A–3), Greer (B–3), Propst (B–12), Colver (C–2), Pickering Bell (D–1), and Helman (D–2).

This outdoor experience of the overland journey had a major effect on women's outlook toward nature. The unknown physical and emotional hazards and weather changes affected how they created their designs. This is evident in the Glover quilts (A–12, 13) made while on the Trail, one with the reference to wind and the other with the reference to wheels.

Quilts made after the Trail experience continued to use nature as a theme, but with a stronger expression and meaning. The Gilfrey quilt (B–16) with its name "Hovering Hawks and Peonies" is the most prominent example. The use of the adjective and noun to describe the triangular shaped birds gives a sense of threat and power to the quilt's meaning. The peony has long been recognized as one of the hardest flowers to transplant, thus adding an increased significance to the wish for recovery.

These shapes and their designs have pattern names that often are easily identifiable. A word of caution is necessary at this point. Including quilt pattern names that are as universally known and widely used as Double Irish Chain and Drunkard's Path does not mean that all quilts using those patterns refer to migration or reflect a woman's Trail experience in the nineteenth century. Instead, if a quilt has these patterns and *all* the other clues point to the time frame of being made within the possible life span of someone who traveled the Trail, then it is probable that the maker wished to express a theme of migration in her quilt. A Drunkard's Path quilt made for The Reverend Enoch and Elizabeth Henderson by their Pennsylvania parishioners was eliminated from the study when it was discovered they came around the Horn to San Francisco in 1856.

The easiest quilts to identify for these themes are those with actual documentation written on the quilt or in supporting notes that accompany them. Usually these have the name and date of someone directly connected to the quilt, and this information is traceable and accurate. This attention to detail by including this information confirms that the makers were using their needles and thread to convey themes meaningful to the events of their lives. The Robbins quilt (B–11), known as the Oregon Rose quilt, has the names and date of the family on it, along with scattered quilted initials, hearts, and wheels. It also is accompanied by extensive written documentation about who made the quilt and when.

Representational Designs

Birds, flowers, leaves, stars, and other objects found in nature have long been used as sources for design in both appliquéd and pieced quilts to express these themes. Quilt historian Elly Sienkiewicz compiled a lexicon of nineteenth-century flowers, birds, and fauna. The sentimental meanings identified for the objects appearing on these quilts are:

Dove: innocence, Holy Spirit, purity, peace—Chambers (A–1), Stone (B–10)
Grape: blood of Christ in the Eucharist—Chambers (A–1)
Hawk: divination—Gilfrey (B–16)
Honeysuckle: devotion, generous affection, mirth, love's bond, "we belong to one another"—Colver (C–2)
Peony: healing—Weaver (B–7), Gilfrey (B–16)

Pine Tree: fidelity, boldness, everlasting life, stability, venerability—Helman (D–2)

Pineapple: hospitality—Gilmour (B–18)

Rose, full blown: "I love you"—Stone (B–10), Robbins (B–11)

Rose of Sharon: romantic love, from Song of Solomon—Foster (A–6)

Star: divine guidance—Chambers (A–1), Riggs (B–1), Gilmour (B–18)

Sunflower: homage, devotion—Stauffer (C–1)

Tulip: renown, fame, spring, dreaminess—Perkins (A–2), Propst (B–12)

Wheel: symbol of divine power—Glover (A–12, A–13)[1]

Many of these objects are included in the seventeen red and green appliqué quilts. This color combination, with added touches of pink, orange, and blue, and the construction dates between 1840 and 1865, corresponds with the general popularity of these quilts with women of the mid-nineteenth century.

The same objects—birds, flowers, stars—are included in some of the thirty-four pieced quilts. Here the design is more by implication through the use of geometric shapes than a representation.

Squares in pieced-pattern quilts give a visual sense of movement through the use of line, defined as the connection between two points. Line has always been an important design element in arts and crafts, for it serves to carry the eye across the design surface. This is especially true with diagonal lines. Nineteenth-century quiltmakers knew this, and they created line by piecing squares and triangles together. Double Irish Chain is made by placing colored squares corner to corner as single units or as units of nine to create lines or chains. Double Nine Patch has the same effect through the use of color to make the line. There are a number of examples in the study, the earliest dating from 1846: Foster quilts (A–5, A–8), Merriman (B–6), and Sawtell (B–14), as well as the Johnson quilt at the Bowman Museum in Prineville.

Triangles are used to represent birds, mountains, and directional movement. Triangles pieced in clusters have been called Birds in Flight in Riddle (B–8) and Hovering Hawks and Peony quilt in Gilfrey (B–16).

The two triangle and peony quilts together carry the message of movement and healing, subtle but encouraging images to someone traveling the Oregon Trail in the 1850s. It is interesting to note that one, Weaver (B–7), was made in 1848, long before the family's migration experience by the aunt or grandmother who did not make the journey. The other, Gilfrey (B–16), was made about fifteen years after the experience of a young daughter traveling with her parents.

Triangles placed in one line are popularly called Wild Goose Chase. The repeat pattern creates a sense of movement from one location to another. The pieced strips are sometimes used in a single line and called Flying Geese as in Weaver (B–7). Other times the strips are used as radiating spokes and called Wild Goose Chase in Fuson (C–5) and Star with Wild Geese in Lieuallen (C–4). This imagery was also used in the writing of the period. John H. Clark wrote in 1852 about his trip to the California gold fields, "I was leaving all that was near and dear to me for a 'wild goose chase.'"[2]

As mountains, triangles in a line appear in Delectable Mountains in Purdom/Leonard (B–2), Setting Sun in Greer (B–3), and Wandering Foot in the Hargrave/Whiteaker (B–4).

Triangles pieced in lines are used to give a sense of direction in Road to California, Drain (B–9).

Rectangles represent fish in Flashing Minnow in Cox (A–15). They represent movement in water and, perhaps, the circumstances surrounding the death of the maker's young husband on the Trail.

Curved pieces, as they appear in the Dibble quilt (B–19) Oregon Trail, is the variation of the popular pattern commonly referred to as Drunkard's Path because of its connection to the Women's Christian Temperance Union. Brackman lists sixty-three names for the twenty-eight different arrangements of the blocks.[3] This quilt made by an Oregon Trail pioneer has a direct connection to this name variation.

Bryan (C–8) was called Bachelor according to family history, also has the variation called Whirlwind connected to movement.

Diamonds as *Stars* have a long history of use in quilt patterns. Here they have a migration theme with reference to divine guidance. Those traveling into the world of the unknown were placing their fate in God's hands, and they asked for help and guidance. An example of this faith would be the Pieced Star quilt (B–18) made by Mary Whitley Gilmour who at age sixty-four came over the Trail in 1852. She was the oldest woman in the study.

The Eight-Pointed Star quilt (C–9) by Ersula Goddard Robison Dean, also called Rolling Star, was noted as a diamond pattern.

The Wheel quilt (A–13) is the name used by Sarah Koontz Glover. While more traditionally referred to as a star pattern, it deserves further exploration.

Wheel Patterns

As an element describing movement and rotation, the wheel is a strong migration theme. Beginning with the nineteenth century meaning of the wheel as a symbol of divine power, it connects with the strong faith these pioneers had in God as they began their journey over the Trail. Their diaries and letters contain many references to God and religion. One of the strongest examples was the prayer found in The Reverend J. H. B. Royal's papers. This prayer was in response to President William Henry Harrison's national request for ministers to pray for an end to the cholera epidemic.

The pioneers depended on wheels to carry them across the plains, and they felt great despair when wheels were broken and a wagonload of precious objects had to be abandoned.

The wheel was important in people's lives to the degree that being a wheelwright, the maker of wheels, was a respected occupation. Royal Hazelton, the father of Amanda Gilfrey (B–16), was a wheelwright. The family history notes the ease with which they joined a wagon train because of his profession.

Once settled, wheels continued to be important in the business of sheltering and feeding a family. Two of the first businesses to be established in the Oregon country were the sawmill and the gristmill, which used wheels to turn the saws and mill stones. Elias Buell, husband of Sarah Hammond. Buell (A–10), established the first mills in Polk County. Eli Perkins, husband of Sally Hull Perkins (A–2), set up the first mills in Yamhill County in the mid 1840s.

Further demonstration of wheels' importance is the recognition that wagon wheels have long been treasures kept and displayed at museums and private homes as symbols of success in the journey across the Plains.

In this project, wheels were pieced or appliquéd into the quilt tops and were also quilted into the design-set or scattered over the surface of the quilts. The pieced quilts include Wheel of Fortune (A–11) made by Lavina E. Frazier Wright in 1848 after her 1843 journey; and Pinwheel (A 12) and Wheel (A–13) pieced during Sarah Koontz Glover's journey westward in 1849. Another appliqué quilt studied for the project with a wheel motif was made by the mother of George W. Starr. He brought it to Oregon in 1876 (after the project's time line) when he was a young man of nineteen. It has red and green circles appliquéd along the border.

Wandering Foot Quilt Pattern

Another pattern name and design important in westward expansion and the Oregon Trail was called Wandering Foot. Today the pattern is more commonly known as Turkey Tracks, whether it is pieced or appliquéd. In this project, it occurred three times in those quilts brought to Oregon between 1850 and 1855 in the Hargrave/Whiteaker (B–4), Patterson (B–5) and Morris (B–13). This is frequently enough to make one question its relationship to migration.

Throughout American pioneer history, wanderlust, the desire to wander, has prompted many men and boys to answer the call for exploration whether for gold, free land, or other riches. The urge to explore and settle the nation was a virtue to be celebrated during the days of building the country. Thus, making a quilt of this pattern was a way of sending a family member off to achieve his country's goals and/or find his fortune.

Exploration was a profession and travel a cultural exercise during the mid-nineteenth century. There were stories of families whose husbands and sons left for the West, not to be heard from for years or perhaps forever.

The pattern was also called Wandering Foot by early twentieth-century quilt book author Ruth Finley. She emphasized gathering the traditional pattern information from the makers in the area of Ohio and the East. Her goal was to make a definitive record of quilts as folk art and an interpretation of them within the time frame of their construction, the nineteenth century. She is now recognized as having gathered the facts, but she romanticized them as myths and legends through her interpretation.[4] This pattern is a case in point. The pattern became mythical with the idea that sleeping under a Wandering Foot would encourage wanderlust and a tendency toward a discontented, unstable, roving disposition. For a young girl, it was a bad influence; for a young boy, it could be fatal. "No bride with an ounce of good sense risked piecing a Wandering Foot for her dower chest." Over the years, though, as communication and transportation methods improved, the name was changed to Turkey Tracks in an effort to dispel the curse and save the quilt pattern.[5]

My supposition is that the name change occurred in the late 1800s when people began to settle down on one piece of property for a longer time, when, through westward migration, they had acquired large enough farms to be able to divide the property among sons and daughters and thus keep them connected to one location. At the same time, job opportunities in new towns were being created, eliminating the need to explore or travel or adventure out to make a living.

The focus of the quilter could turn from the worry and sadness brought on by the departure of family members to the challenges of operating a homestead and farm. The tasks of tending the chickens, milking the cows, and caring for the geese and turkeys became women's work as men tended to work in the fields or off the farm. The ongoing task of keeping track of wandering turkeys could now be expressed humorously in a quilt pattern. The vision of four turkeys fleeing in four directions at one time is clear in the pattern's design.

While a number of quilts called Turkey Tracks are found in collections today, most likely they were contributed without a name or were given one that was contemporary to the cataloger's or donor's life rather than the maker's. Some of the cotton quilts with the name Turkey Tracks on the inventory cards are actually Wandering Foot, made in the period when exploration and wanderlust were considered something important a boy had to accomplish to become a man.

Log Cabin

The pieced quilt pattern group called Log Cabin has long been a symbol of new land and settlement. To make the quilt, strips of fabrics or "logs" are stitched around a center square, building one upon another until the block size is complete. Two wool quilts were part of the project. One was made by Grace Simpson Skeeters (B–22) years later after her migration in 1853. The other, not included in the book, is a brown and blue one made by Margaret Bailey (1830–1907) in the 1860s prior to her move from Illinois to Oregon. It is part of the Junction City Historical Museum collection at Junction City.

Quilting Designs

The stitched lines used to hold the layers of the quilt together often carry meaning in their designs and symbols. Among these quilts, the following arrangement of quilting designs exists.

Scattered. This term refers to random placement over the surface of the quilt. This was a format often used with appliqué quilts of the mid-nineteenth century. Hearts, wheels, stems of flowers, and leaves, as well as initials and dates, are there, often to be discovered by the curious eye. These are the clues within the quilt regarding date, people, and meanings. Often more than one of these motifs occurs in a quilt. For instance, there are wheels in five quilts: Buell

(A–10), Robbins (B–11), Stauffer (C–1), Colver (C–2), and Mills (C–5).

Block by block. In the period 1850 to 1870, quilt designs had moved away from the whole cloth, central medallion, or large appliqué blocks to the format of smaller pieced blocks. The appearance of the quilting designs changed with the advent of a block-by-block repeat of a quilting design. This design is often a wreath or sunflower. Quilts with this format include: Merriman (B–6), Sawtell (B–14), Gilmour (B–18), and Aurora Colony (C–10).

The Weaver quilt (B–7) and the Pickering Bell quilt (D–1) have the additional feature of stuffwork. As the quilting was completed, the petals of the wreaths and the pieces of fruit were stuffed with cotton to give extra height and visual appeal.

All-over. Quilting styles began to change from elaborate close quilting and stuffing to simpler forms as demands on women's time increased or as they grew older. They began to use faster ways of drawing patterns and designs easier to mark and quilt. All-over patterns of straight lines and grid work placed equal distance apart were drawn and quilted. The Cox (A–15) and Lieuallen quilts (C–3) are examples.

The curved lines of elbow/fan quilting were also easy to place for quilting. A series of marks was spaced equidistant along a board. As the lines were needed, the elbow was placed on the appropriate mark and the line drawn as the arm swung the curve across the quilt. A number of the quilts have this style including: Foster (A–7), Wright (A–11), Morris (B–13), Giesy (B–15), and Fuson (C–5).

The third style, where the quilting line echoes the line of the pieced pattern, is called echo. Additional lines fill in the space, either repeating the pattern of the first or establishing a gridwork. The Foster quilt (A–9) employed this format.

Using this research data and conclusions as a guide, clues are now available to study other migration-related quilts. Owners and families are encouraged to compare their treasures with those found in trunks of families, museums, and historical societies, lovingly preserved and interpreted for an interested and caring public. Enjoy them as the opportunities present themselves during the next thirty years of celebrating of the Oregon Trail's Sesquicentennial Anniversary.

APPENDIX B *Triumphs and Tragedies: Letters and Narrations of the Oregon Trail Experience*

THE FOLLOWING LETTERS AND NARRATIONS are ones collected during this research that enrich the understanding of the experience in terms of women and their quilts.

They are arranged chronologically, along with brief explanations. They are printed "as found" with original spelling and punctuation. Several are in private collections and are being published here for the first time.

Triumph

THE 1846 JOURNEY AND OREGON EXPERIENCE OF TABITHA MOFFETT BROWN

One of the most famous women in Oregon history who used her needlework skills to establish herself and achieve her goal was Tabitha Moffett Brown now recognized by the state as the Mother Symbol of Oregon, representative of the distinctive pioneer heritage and the charitable and compassionate nature of Oregon's people.

Born in Brimfield, Massachusetts, on May 1, 1780, she married The Reverend Clark Brown about 1799. After he died in Maryland in 1817, leaving her with two sons and one daughter, she moved to Missouri where she organized and successfully ran a school. At the age of sixty-six she crossed the Plains in 1846 with her son, Orus Brown, and his wife and eight children; her daughter, Pherne Brown Pringle, and her husband and five children; and her brother-in-law, seventy-seven-year-old Captain John Brown, for whom she

Tabitha Moffett Brown

143

had kept house after her husband had died thirty years earlier. Completing a long and difficult journey of nine months, she arrived in the Willamette Valley. Part of her difficulty was a leg paralysis requiring the use of a cane.

In a letter which she wrote to her brother and sister in August 1854, Tabitha Brown reviewed her journey West and told of the school she started:

On Christmas day at 2 P.M. I entered the house of a Methodist minister, the first house I had set my feet in for nine months. For two or three weeks of my journey down the Willamette I had felt something in the end of my glove finger which I supposed to be a button. On examination at my new home in Salem, I found it to be a six and a quarter cent piece. This was the whole of my cash capital to commence business with in Oregon. With it I purchased three needles. I traded off some of my old clothes to the squaws for buck skins, worked them into gloves for the Oregon ladies and gentlemen, which cleared me upwards of thirty dollars.

Later I accepted the invitation of Mr. and Mrs. Clark of Tualatin Plains to spend the winter with them. I said to Mr. Clark one day, "Why has Providence frowned on me and left me poor in this world? Had He blessed me with riches as He has many others, I know right well what I would do." "What would you?" "I would establish myself in a comfortable house and receive all poor children and be a mother to them." He fixed his keen eyes upon me to see if I were in earnest. "Yes, I am," said I. "If so, I will try," said he, "to help you." He proposed to take an agency and get assistance to establish a school in the plain. I should go into the old log meeting house, and receive all the children, rich and poor. Those parents who were able were to pay one dollar a week for board, tuition, washing and all. I agreed to labor one year for nothing, while Mr. Clark and others were to assist as far as they were able in furnishing provisions. The time fixed upon to begin was March, 1848, when I found everything prepared for me to go into the old meeting house and cluck up my chickens. The neighbors had collected what broken knives and forks, tin pans and dishes they could part with, for the Oregon pioneer to commence housekeeping with. I had a well educated lady from the East, a missionary's wife, for a teacher and my family increased rapidly. In the summer they put me up a boarding house. I now had thirty boarders, of both sexes and of all ages, from four years old to twenty-one. I managed then and did all my work except washing. That was done by the scholars.

In the spring of '49, we called for trustees. Had eight appointed. They voted me the whole charge of the boarding house free of rent and I was to provide for myself. The price of board was established at two dollars per week. Whatever I made over my expenses was my own. In '51 I had forty in my family at two dollars and fifty cents per week; mixed with my own hands 3,423 pounds of flour in less than five months. Mr. Clark made over to the trustees a quarter section of land for a town plat. A large and handsome building is on the site that we selected at the first starting. It has been under town incorporation for two years and at the last session of the legislature a charter was granted for a university, to be called Pacific University, with a limitation of $50,000. The president and professor are already here from Vermont. The teacher and his lady for the academy are from New York.

I have endeavored to give general outlines of what I have done. You must be judges, whether I have been doing good or evil. I have labored for myself and the rising generation. But I have not quit hard work and live at my ease, independent as to worldly concerns. I own a nicely finished white frame house, on a lot in town, within a short distance of the public buildings. That I rent for $100 per year. I have eight other town lots without buildings worth $150 each. I have eight cows and a number of young cattle. The cows I rent out for their milk and one-half of their increase. I have rising $1,100 cash due me. $400 of it I have donated to the university, besides $100 I gave to the academy three years ago. This much I have been able to accumulate by my own industry, independent of my children, since I drew six and a quarter scents [sic] from the finger of my glove.[6]

Tragedy and Triumph

THE 1847 JOURNEY AND OREGON EXPERIENCE OF ELIZABETH GEER

Her life was one of terrible tragedy and delightful triumph as reflected in her diary and letters. For Elizabeth Geer, the arrival in Oregon City was bleak, with a sick husband, seven children, and a bed:

November 30. Raining. This morning I ran about trying to get a house to get into with my sick husband. At last I found a small, leaky concern with two families already in it. . . you could have stirred us with a stick. . . . My children and I carried up a bed. The distance was nearly a quarter of a mile. Made it down on the floor in the mud. I got some men to carry my husband up through the rain and lay him on it and he was never out of that shed until he was carried out in his coffin. Here lay five of us bedfast at one time and we had no money and what few things we had left that would bring money I had to sell. I had to give ten cents a pound for fresh pork, seventy-five cents a bushel for potatoes and four cents a pound for fish. There are so many of us sick that I can not write any more. . . .

January 15, 1848. My husband is still alive, but very sick. There is no medicine here except at Fort Vancouver, and the people there will not sell one bit—not even a bottle of wine.

January 31. Rain all day. If I could tell you how we suffer you would not believe it. Our house, or rather a shed joined to a house, leaks all over. The roof descends in such a manner that the rain runs right down into the fire. I have dipped as much as six pails of water off our dirt hearth in one night. Here I sit up night after night with my poor sick husband, all alone, and expecting him every day to die. . . . I have not undressed to lie down for six weeks. Besides our sickness I had a cross little babe to care of. Indeed, I cannot tell you half.

February 1. Rain all day. This day my dear husband, my last remaining friend, died.

February 2. Today we buried my earthly companion. Now I know what none but widows know: that is, how comfortless is a widow's life; especially when left in a strange land without money or friends, and the care of seven children.[7]

Butteville, Oregon Ty., Yamhill County, Sept. 2, 1850.

Dear and Estimable Friends,
Mrs. Paulina Foster and Mrs. Cynthia Ames:
   I promised when I saw you last to write to you when I got to Oregon, and I done it faithfully, but as I never have received an answer, I do not know whether you got my letter and diary or not, consequently I do not know what to write now. I wrote four sheets full and sent it to you, but now I have not time to write. I write now to know whether you got my letter; and I will try to state a few things again. My husband was taken sick before we got to any settlement, and never was able to walk afterwards. He died at Portland, on the Willamette River, after an illness of two months. I will not attempt to describe my troubles since I saw you. Suffice it to say that I was left a widow with the care of seven children in a foreign land, without one solitary friend, as one might say, in the land of the living; but this time I will only endeavor to hold up the bright side of the picture. I lived a widow one year and four months. My three boys started for the gold mines, and it was doubtful to me whether I ever saw them again. Perhaps you will think it strange that I let such young boys go; but I was willing and helped them off in as good style as I could. They packed through by land. Russell Welch went by water. The boys never saw Russell in the mines. Well after the boys were gone, it is true I had plenty of cows and hogs and plenty of wheat to feed them on and to make my bread. Indeed, I was well off if I had only known it; but I lived in a remote place where my strength was of little use to me. I could get nothing to do, and you know I could not live without work. I employed myself in teaching my children: yet that did not fully occupy my mind. I became as poor as a snake, yet I was in good health, and never was so nimble since I was a child. I could run a half a mile without stopping to breathe. Well, I thought perhaps I had better try my fortune again; so on the 24th of June, 1849,

I was married to a Mr. Joseph Geer, a man 14 years older than myself, though young enough for me. He is the father of ten children. They are all married, but two boys and two girls. He is a Yankee from Connecticut and he is a Yankee in every sense of the word, as I told you he would be if it ever proved my lot to marry again. I did not marry rich, but my husband is very industrious, and is as kind to me as I can ask. Indeed, he sometimes provokes me for trying to humor me so much. He is a stout, healthy man for one of his age.

The boys made out poorly at the mines. They started in April and returned in September, I think. They were sick part of the time and happened to be in poor diggings all the while. They only got home with two hundred dollars apiece. They suffered very much while they were gone. When they came home they had less than when they started. Perley did not get there. He started with a man in partnership. The man was to provide for and bring him back, and he was to give the man half he dug; but when they got as far as the Umpqua River, they heard it was so very sickly there that the man turned back; but Perley would not come back. There were two white men keeping ferry on the Umpqua, so Perley stayed with them all summer and in the fall he rigged out on his own hook and started again; but on his way he met his brothers coming home, and they advised him for his life not to go, and so he came back with them.

At this time we are all well but Perley. I cannot answer for him; he has gone to the Umpqua for some money due him. The other two are working for four dollars a day. The two oldest boys have got three town lots in quite a stirring place called Lafayette in Yamhill County. Perley has four horses. A good Indian horse is worth one hundred dollars. A good American cow is worth sixty dollars. My boys live about 25 miles from me, so that I cannot act in the capacity of a mother to them; so you will guess it is not all sunshine with me, you know my boys are not old enough to do without a mother. Russell Welch done very well in the mines. He made about twenty hundred dollars. He lives 30 miles below me in a little town called Portland on the Willamette River. Sarah has got her third son. It has been one year since I saw her. Adam Polk's two youngest boys live about wherever they see fit. The oldest, if he is alive, is in California. There is some ague in this country this season, but neither I nor my children, except those that went to California, have had a day's sickness since we came to Oregon.

I believe I will say no more until I hear from you. Write as soon as possible and tell me everything. My husband will close this epistle.

—Elizabeth Geer.

Butteville, Sept. 9, 1850.

Dear Ladies:

As Mrs. Geer has introduced me to you, as her old Yankee husband, I will say a few words, in the hope of becoming more acquainted hereafter. She so often speaks of you, that you seem like old neighbors. She has neglected to tell you that she was once the wife of Cornelius Smith. She has told you how poor she became while a widow, but has not said one word about how fat she has become since she has been living with her Yankee husband. This is probably reserved for the next epistle, so I will say nothing about it.

Of her I will only say she makes me a first-rate wife, industrious, and kind almost to a fault to me, a fault, however, that I can cheerfully overlook, you know.

We are not rich, but independent, and live agreeably together, which is enough. We are located on the west bank of the Willamette River, about 20 miles above Oregon City, about 40 yards from the water—a very pleasant situation. Intend putting out a large orchard as soon as I can prepare the ground; have about ten thousand apple trees, and about 200 pear trees on hand. Trees for sale of the best kinds of fruit. Apple trees worth one dollar, and pears $1.50 apiece. I have not room to give you a description of this, the best country in the world, so I will not attempt it; but if you will answer this I will give you a more particular account next time. I will give a brief account of myself. I left my native home, Windham, Conn., Sept. 10, 1818, for Ohio; lived in Ohio till Sept. 9, 1840, when I left for Illinois. Left Illinois April 4, 1847, for Oregon; arrived here Oct. 18, 1847. Buried my first wife Dec. 6, 1847.

Now I wish you or some of your folks to write to us and let us know all about the neighbors, as Mrs. Geer is very anxious to hear from you all.

Direct to Joseph C. Geer, Sen., Butteville, Marion County, Oregon Territory.

My best respects to Mr. Ames, and if there is a good Universalist preacher there, tell him he would meet with a cordial welcome here, as there is not one in this Territory.

I must close for want of room.

Yours respectfully,

Joseph C. Geer, Sen.

Mrs. P. Foster, and Mrs. C. Ames.

Triumph

THE JOURNEY AND 1850 OREGON EXPERIENCE OF C. C. PARRISH AND WIFE

This letter was written to friends back East, telling of their accomplishments in Oregon and their solutions to the challenges of the journey. As such, it is a personal statement on their dreams and the measure of their success. The letter is from the collection of Wanita Propst Haugen, owner of Quilt B–12.

Near Syracuse Marion County, Oregon Territory

Nov. 15th, 1850

Hugh & Sarepta Nickerson der Children
By this you may see that we still live, it is by the mercy of a kinde & indulgent Heavenly father that we are thus faivored.

Seven long years have hastened away since we took the parting
hand with our friends upon the old walks of Ohio, to go, we
then knew not where, but our kind guide conducted us safely to
this good land, and now may we not inquire, what shall we
render to God for all his benefeits. Oh, what cause of
thankfulness have we, seeing that we all live, and enjoy life, and
the bounties of a good providence. While we are continually
hearing of the doings of the monster Death, and, notwithstanding, we feelingly condole with our friends in their losses and
bereavments, yet, we all have cause to thank God that it is no
worse; for when we morne, not as those do, who have no hope,
we find in the cup of sorrow, a mixture of joy which nothing but
the religion of Jeasus can inspire. O, then let us lean on the
Saviour for support, and all will be well—As for my familly, we
have nothing to complain of except our own unworthyness, and
not much to desire that we have not, except it is religion and the
means of grace, we have long looked and desired to see the day
when some of our good preachers would come to our releaf.
And we are now cheered with prospect and are beginning to
sing. There is a better day a coming—we are pleased to here that
our friends are waking up to a sence of their own intrust in view
of coming to this country, the best we honestly believe on this
side of Heaven. When we try to discribe it, we fall short about
half way, yet the people of the States think it is romance.
Business is now verry lively in this territory. Markets are pretty
good. Jackson and his mother has just returned from Oregon Ct.
with the team. They sold 23 bushels of onions at seven dollars
per bushel, 126 pounds of butter at one dollar per pound, 24
hed of cabages at fifty cents per hed, 14 bushels of oats at two
dollars per bushel—Beets were worth four dollars per bushel but
they took none with them—They bought good calico at 12½
cents per yd by the bolt. Bleached muslin at 18 cents pr yd by
the bolt. Brown muslin at the same. Sugar at 18 cts. per pound,
salt 4 cents per pound. We sold our peaches this year at six
dollars pr bushel and from .25 to .50 pr doz. In this way we
took in some 300 dollars. Potatoes are worth three dollars at the
Citty, but we have sold them at home this year for one dollar,
and as low as fifty cts, they are plenty here now, for all the prices
are so high, yet provisions of all kinds are exceding by plenty for
every boddy, hereabouts. I wish to say to you, and threw you to
all my relations and old acquaintances that we are prepairing to
supply you with provisions, on the cheepest terms, we have
already planted considerable many potatoes, and but for the
school, we should be at it today, as the weather is fine. While I
am writing I look out at the window upon the prairies and fields
and they remind me of your middle of May. The emigrants have
bin coming in, more or less for two months, their stock is poor,
but all they have to do is to let them loos and look after them a
little and they soon come out of the kinks. A large portion of
this years Emigration started for California, but on hearing of
the grass being burned of on that road they turned for Oregon,
but being so verry late in the season, fall raines came on, then
snow caught them in the Cascade Mountains. Much of their
stock died, they had to leav Waggons and all behind, and be
carried out on hors back. O, take warning of this, start early on

Brother Clancies plan, and when you start, press on, be fourmost if possible. You may be here by the tenth of August at farthest, then you may bring in your stock in good condition, weather dry and pleasant—bring your beads and clothing with plenty of provision. Feather beds are harder to come at then anything els, if I was Hugh & Mc. I would bring a small box of small tools, such as match plains and the like with plain bits, as timber is plenty in Oregon. Broad axes, addzes, augers and the like are plenty and of good quality. I wish Hugh and_____and the friends to help McClure to a deacent outfit so that he may bring his familly along with the rest of the friends as comfortably and as independantly as the rest, having his own Wagon and team, and I will take it as a faivour, and will refund the money on your arrival at my place. The propper way will be to take his note or receit and present it to me, as I cannot bare the idea of having him left—I want to say a word on a dilicate subject. It is this—it sometimes comes to pass that we are admonished that before we can posably get threw this long journey that we must have an increas of family, and of cours we cannot go this season, now for the information of all such, we can inform you that we had a great many such ocurances in our Emigration and are prepaired to say that we a whole, we never knew Mothers and infants to do better, our frolicks mostly came on in the nite, and when the signs of the times indicated a storm it was easy to select a suitable place in the incampment and we were always ready to role out in the morning with the company—I want to say a word about the journey, that it is long and tiresom, is a matter none of ya need doubt, but if you can keep health, the continual occurance of knew objects will make the time pass along more agreeably—how to preserve health, in ordinary seasons you will not be likely to git sick if you conduct with prudence untill you reach the great Plat River. This river is like no other River, perhaps in the world, it is made by the streams of the Rocky Mountains, water pure at first, but is flows down with a courant bold and majestic, its bed is sand and that continually, conciquently, the water is muddy, looks like it is not fit for man or beast to drink. To avoid this dificulty, our Emigration resorted to well diging with a spade. You can dig a well two or three feet deep in a few minutes when clean water imediately comes in plenty, this practice became general, and the conciquence was we soon had sickness plenty, the River water is the best by far, and you should avoid those stink holes as you would avoid poison. Now friends I wish you to take this advise, provide buckets or other vesels sufficient to hold water nough to do you threw the night and some to put in your water bag in the morning, by standing threw the night it settles with the sand at the bottom— but if you put a little sweet milk in the water, it settles in a few minits reddy for use, take this cours and plenty of good Cayanne and Labelici, with the blessing of God and industry and you may get threw in good time and perhaps better health than when you started—One word more for McClure, we wish him and his familly to take courage. I think he will get money before you get this, as James R. Robb (a good fellow) has written to his partner at New York to send him money, but if he should not git it in that way, let the friends who can, advance it for him doubting not Robb, Gamahil and myself all stand readdy and pledged to refund the cash on sight, my wish is that you take pains to let this paper have a circulation among all the friends—my opinyan is that prices will be a little reduced by the time you arive, but if prices should keep up, all the better, as it will soon be your turn to sell to others—This is the easiest place to make a living, to make property, or even cash if you pleas that you ever saw—My sheet is now full, I must bid you fairwell for a while, be sure, write when you start from Misoury and tel us know who is coming.

—C. C. Parrish & Wife.

to Hugh & Sarepta Nickerson

Tragedy and Triumph

THE 1851 JOURNEY AND EXPERIENCE OF ESTHER MCMILLAN HANNA

One journal that graphically describes the end of the journey for a young, energetic eighteen-year-old woman is that of Esther McMillan Hanna. She mentions using a quilt and later staying in a cabin where the dying man is the husband of Lucinda Powell Propst (Quilt B–12). She and her husband, The Reverend Joseph A. Hanna, left Pittsburgh, Pennsylvania, within an hour of their wedding ceremony for the trip across the country to establish the second Presbyterian church in Oregon at Marysville, now called Corvallis. After six months, Esther is exhausted and frail when the following entry picks up. They have come down Laurel Hill on the west slope of Mount Hood and are headed to "Foster's place."

Wednesday, 15th. Last night it commenced raining about midnight. We were lying out with a quilt and two blankets. We got up, put our sack containing a few personal things under Mr. H.'s gum coat. We then hoisted our umbrella over our heads, lay down again and slept! This morning our quilt was wet through and all our clothing damp. We had a hard bed as the ground was very uneven, with nothing but a blanket under us. I felt very sore and my limbs were stiff from the effects of walking so far yesterday and the damp of last night. . . . I burst into a flood of tears. It seemed that trouble and trials came thick and fast upon us, and at a time when we could least bear it. Mr. H. tried to comfort me although he was so much agitated as to be hardly able to speak. We started on again with troubled hearts and weary feet.

Thursday, 16th. We all slept comfortably and arose this morning in fine spirits, as we hope to reach the valley today. . . . Part of our road this day was good and part very bad, having some steep ascents and descents to make. Got along fairly well and about four o'clock we came in sight of houses and gardens, fields and fences! My heart arose in gratitude to God that we had been spared to reach this land! Six long months have elapsed since we left our native land, and now after having passed through dangers seen and unseen, sickness, trial and difficulty, toil and fatigue, we are safely landed on the Pacific shores! Thus far the Lord has led us on. "Hitherto He has helped us. What shall we render unto His name for his goodness unto us?"

Saturday, 18th. . . . have become quite domesticated in our little cabin. Have been baking and cooking all afternoon! The sick man in the other room is in a dying state. He has been insensible since yesterday. No friends near him but his oldest, a lad of 14. The rest of his children, 4 in number, having been sent on up the valley, 30 miles to an uncle. He was a man of property in Illinois, but owing to the persuasion of his wife, who wished to come here to her brother, at her solicitation, he sold all and came West. She died of fever on the Umatilla river, and he is dying here alone among strangers, lying on a pallet of straw with no kind friend to smooth his pillow! His brother-in-law has not yet arrived. There is a great deal of sickness and distress in the mountains. Every team here lost more or less of their cattle. Some have even lost all and have been obliged to leave their wagons and all. Some are entirely out of provisions and a great number are sick—almost every wagon that comes in have sick in it!

Sabbath, 19th. The poor emigrant in the next room died at 3 this morning. His brother-in-law came last evening with a carriage expecting to take him home, little thinking that he was so near his long home. Persons in the states would think it awful to see the near relations of the deceased lay out the corpse, clothe it, dig the grave and assist in filling it up again. But I witnessed that sad sight today! . . . The coffin was of plain boards, unpainted and unlined. The corpse was shroudless with but a checked shirt and drawers. Before lifting the corpse, Mr. H. attended to singing and prayer, making a few appropriate remarks. We then attended the remains to their resting place. It was a heart-breaking time for all of us![8]

Tragedy

THE LOST WAGON TRAIN OF 1853 EXPERIENCE OF LUCINDA ANN LEONARD WORTH'S FAMILY

The Lost Wagon Train of 1853 involved two of the quilts in this study, Purdom/Leonard quilt (B–2) and Harlow quilt (A–16). Over 1,500 emigrants chose to follow the suggestion of Elijah Elliott to cut miles off the journey by heading into the southern end of the Willamette Valley, a journey taken at great risk. Because of the number of unknowns, many became lost in the rugged Cascade Mountains for up to two months. The personal accounts of families who took this route indicate the eagerness to get to their destination before the weather changed and the supplies ran out.

Many Oregonians of today can trace their family's involvement in this experience as either victims or rescuers. There are several other quilts in this project that connect with families who were a part of the fateful trip. "The Joseph Leonards were with the Millers, and the McClures nearby."[9] The young couple, Alan and Rachel Bond, who brought only what they could carry, including a bundle of fabrics, were with the McClure party.

Francis Burris Tandy Harlow, maker of the album quilt with the names of her daughters and granddaughters, was one of the rescuers organizing her family and neighbors to pack a wagon full of supplies, food, and clothing.[10]

The story of this particular train's experience reflects the desperation many people faced after having been as long as five months on the Trail, always seeking water and food for livestock, fresh supplies for themselves, and respite from the long journey's toll of boredom, dust, illness, and death. It also illustrates the risks they took following new leads to better supplies and for shorter travel times. Information was passed on by word of mouth, often without personal knowledge by the speaker. Such was the case here.

Elijah Elliott, the leader of the train, had come West in 1852 traveling with the largest wagon migration movement ever to cross the Trail. He left his wife and family in Illinois with the plan to stake his claim in Oregon and then to fetch them the following year. Settling in Lane County, near Eugene, he saw the new town being planned and heard talk of the new road being charted over the Cascades to lead people to the area. He was assured by the planners that the road would be blazed by autumn. He also had heard that Joe Meek had come that way in 1845; but he did not know the degree of difficulty that Meek had encountered, wandering for weeks to find a way across the mountains. Going to meet his family at Fort Boise, he experienced an area of central and eastern Oregon's mountains, flats, alkali lakes, and deserts where he had never been. He was perplexed by the experience and recommended the group go north around the lakes. There was disagreement among the other leaders and Elliott was overruled. He led the group south through the marshes and deserts, taking up to three weeks to travel a distance of a few dozen miles.[11]

Catherine Leonard Jones, the granddaughter of Katherine Purdom, who made Quilt B–2, recorded the experience of the Leonard family in a letter:

Marquam, Oregon, November 12, 1903

All went nicely until we came to Malheur River about eighteen miles this side of Snake River. There we met a man that came to meet his family, his wife and his two lovely children who were traveling with us. He had been in Oregon two years and told us of a road that was two hundred miles nearer and we could get good feed for our poor worn out teams. This was the first of September. Well, Father thought if Mr. Elliott was willing to risk his family that he must be telling the truth, so we consented to go with him. We gathered three large trains of forty wagons in each and we started into the Blue Mountains. We kept on old Meek's road that was traveled in 1845 or 46 until we crossed the Blue Mountains, then we came to chalk and glass mountains or hills. When we came in sight of the lake which I suppose is Harney Lake, Mr. Elliott said we must go south, so we left the road and went to the south of the lake. You may be sure that we had a hard time traveling without a road through Indian country. . . .

We went around the lake and then struck out on a barren desert, nothing but sagebrush and sometimes a spot of wild onions. Plenty of water in the winter, I suppose, but in October when we came through, it was dry as ashes. We traveled on this desert all day and night long and in the morning when our teams gave out we loosened them from the wagons and the men took kegs on their backs and followed the cattle about ten miles and found water. We had to stay there six days for the teams to get so they could come back to the wagons. The men went every day and brought water to drink. When we started from there we went by the little stream and stopped all night and then went on across another desert, but were more cautious about filling our canteens.

At the first desert I saw a lot of men draw up two wagons and tie the end of the tongues together, they said they were going to hang Mr. Elliott for leading us through that road. Father, Mother and several of the men begged them to spare his life. He admitted he did not know anything about the road but thought it was all right and claimed that the people in the upper end of the valley said they would pay him five hundred dollars to pilot the emigrants through that way. He offered all his cattle to be killed for food for the starving people for we were without flour or anything to eat. Everyone that was sick died. . . . After we crossed the second desert, we could see three snow peaks in the distance which were the Three Sisters and came to an old Indian trail to Fall River or Deschutes. . . .

Here we stayed six days hunting a road: finally we started up the river, traveled about forty miles, then forded it. Now here was a place that we out-fitted those two younger men to go for assistance. It was then in November. People threw in and bought an old mare, then gave them dried meat and bedclothes and they started not knowing what was before them. Here the snow fell; we went through six inches of snow, it was terribly cold and wet; we crossed the summit. Oh! such a road, here we found a grindstone that showed someone had been here. The road was cut in some places; they had bridged over logs four feet through rather than cut them out; the suffering was intense as we came down the Willamette; the stream was narrow and swift and we could ford it every little while; every time it was a little deeper until the last time Father said we could not make it.

We were near it, sitting down eating boiled beef straight when two men came riding up to us, threw us down some flour and potatoes, never was morsel more gladly received. The boys had taken in word of starving people. . . . That night the citizens of that place made up five hundred dollars of provisions for the emigrants. And plenty of men and pack animals loaded with provisions went out after us. Every man, when his pack was unloaded, would take some of the emigrants on their horses to the valley.[12]

Treasure

THE 1855 OREGON EXPERIENCE OF JOHN BRUCE BELL

This treasure found among the family items of Mary Carpenter Pickering (Quilt D–1) was a letter written by John Bruce Bell from Oregon in 1855. The letter is charming and exhibits much of the sentiment about the Oregon Territory in the mid-1850s and what separation from friends meant.

Plum Valley, Polk County, O.T. May 21st, 1855

Friend Mary

It has been a long time since I received your letter, and I really feel ashamed to think that I have so long neglected to answer. I have no excuse but think not Mary that you were forgotten. I can never cease to remember all the friends so linked together when fond memory brings the light of the other days around me. Though far separated and in a strange land with none of the friends of my youth around, to cheer or with whom I can talk over the merry times when were boys together, how can I then forget. No, while I have a heart to feel, and memory carries me back to the scenes of old Belmont you shall be ever cherished as one worthy and bright spot in my memory. I sometimes wish myself back once more, when I think of the friends I left behind and the many hallowed associations which made them dear to me, of the many pleasures, and of all and everything which were once so familiar to me. I almost wish I had never left and often long to return.

We had a very mild pretty winter. There was no cold weather of any consequence. Spring with all her charms, is now upon us, and all Oregon is now clothed in her richest robes. At no time does this country look prettier. The prairies are covered with flowers. It is still showery, and the grass is much better this spring than I have ever seen it. I am in hopes that we will have dry weather all the time before long. We will soon have plenty of fruit. Peaches do not do well here. I think it is rather too cool during the summer for them, but I think this will be a great country for apples. There is but a few orchards of grafted fruit bearing yet, but you will scarcely find a farm, which has not a large orchard planted, and it will not be long until we shall have plenty of fruit. I have not had two dozen apples since I left the states. There is none about here and when they are, they sell at from ten to fifteen dollars per bushel. We have no wild fruit, except berries, and I do not know how many kinds of berries there are here but I know there are some which I never saw in the states. Strawberries are ripe now and are very plenty. I was out with the women this forenoon. They promised to give me a strawberry dinner if I would go out and help them gather. Well I went, but it was a great sacrifice for me to put any in a vessel when they look so tempting and seemed to say eat me. I thought when I was out, that if it had been yourself and Sister Marth, instead of two O. women I would have seen more pleasure. I wish there was a band of the Buckeye girls here, I would like to take a romp over these hills and have them for company. It is well enough however to please the old women occasionally, and get a little into their good graces by minding the little Oregonians and other little chores, and then a person can ask little favors such as sewing on a button and such like little things with a better face. I believe I have told you something about the girls here. Well I have not fallen in love with any of them yet. There are but very few that have come to years of accountability and they act as though they never saw anything in their lives but their parents. I do not know from experience but fellows who have tried visiting them, say the only place they can be found is behind the door, whither they flee to avoid the sight of man. Well I will make allowance for them. They have been raised up in a new country have had no opportunities for education and are not accustomed to society and have had a poor chance. But still I think they should have sense enough not to marry so soon. If they would only wait till they were eighteen or twenty they would be of some account. Well there is no danger of me robbing any of the cradles here while I keep my senses. I suppose that of the girls of my acquaintances have married and I did expect to hear that you had gone and done likewise and I know not but that you are gone or going. Well I hope there will be some left until I return and I will not let many years roll round until I bid welcome to my native hills once more. Young men are plenty here and a great many have about the same opinion of the girls as I have, and intent to go back. I like the people here better now than at first. They are mostly Missourians, and have not time to describe one to you, but they have been raised among slaves, and you can guess what they are like. What Buckeyes that are here are the best citizens we have, and if Oregon was settled with them it would be the best place in the world. Oregon is very healthy but very little ague and that only in some places. I had a letter from Marth lately I would like to see her so much, she is always so kind and good humored. I have no heard from Nancy lately. I think she must have a notion of getting married. Well I must go home and see all the folks before long or I will forget how they all looked. I could spend a few months in Ohio now with pleasure. But is no use to regret. I am here and I can't help it now, only by going back when I can. Give my love and respects to all, and may I ask you to write

soon, and to not do as I have done. And now I must bid you
good bye, asking to be remembered by you, and with wishes for
your welfare and happiness hoping that nothing will mar the
smooth current of your life, I still remain your friend in Oregon.

Mary C. Pickering   Good Bye   J. B. Bell of Belmont[13]

Triumph

THE STORY OF THE DARNING NEEDLE OWNED BY NANCY GATES ENSLEY DRAIN (QUILT B–9)

The triumphant story about the darning needle is part of Oregon
folklore. It was told and retold and eventually recorded in *With
Her Own Wings,* a collection of sketches about pioneer women
compiled by Portland's Federation of Women's Organizations.

The Darning Needle Story

This is an example of pioneer folklore, a story told and re-told
by old-timers. Most of the story was told by Mary Drain Albro
of Portland. Howard M. Corning has verified enough of the facts
to convince us that the incident could have occurred in 1852 or
1853.

Grandmother Drain had a darning needle, and it was the only
darning needle among the settlers in Pass Creek Canyon.

The folks who lived in Pass Creek Canyon had come across the
plains by wagon train. By the time they got to the top of the
Cascades, they were so eager to end their journey they settled at
the first likely spots as they went down the west slopes. Every
natural clearing close to water was the site of a land claim. Pass
Creek Canyon was quite thickly settled, at least there were ten or
fifteen families living within a few miles of each other, and they
neighbored back and forth, sharing what they had. In those days
families had to get along with each other. No one knew when he
might need help.

Grandmother Drain's darning needle was one of the most
cared-for possessions in the community, because it was the only
one, and clothes had to be patched and mended until new ones
could be secured, and who knew when that would be? The
women learned to make pins out of slivers of dogwood, but for
mending nothing was so handy to use as the darning needle.

Women in the lower canyon shared the needle for a day or
two, then women up farther would take turns catching up on the
family mending.

All went well until the day Mrs. Chitwood sent the needle
back to Grandmother Drain's by Jimmy.

Jimmy was eight years old, and he was a responsible boy—
boys had to be responsible and do their share of the work.

Oregonian *Meier and Frank*
advertisement, January 1, 1967

Mrs. Chitwood put a long red raveling through the eye of the needle and knotted it, then she put the needle into a potato so that Jimmy could carry it safely to the Drain cabin.

Jimmy walked through the canyon trail in the spring morning sunshine which filtered through the tall firs. He paid no attention to rabbits and squirrels that crossed the path in front of him. He scarcely looked up when bluejays scolded. He stopped for a moment when a doe raced a few yards down the trail as though being chased, but he did not leave the trail. He was on an errand with the only darning needle in Pass Creek Canyon.

But when a mother bear with two cubs came into sight, he jumped from the trail and hid behind a serviceberry bush to watch them. He was not afraid, he said to himself, because bears didn't harm, but of course a mother bear was different when she had cubs. No, he was not afraid, but it was best to hide just the same. He stood behind the bush, then stooped down. It would be nice, he thought, if Father were here to see the bears, too. He was not afraid, but he wished the bears would hurry along on their way. And after a bit they did.

Jimmy stood up again and went back onto the trail. He walked a little, thinking of the bears and wishing that sometime he might have a cub all his own, without a mother bear.

Then he remembered the darning needle! He looked down at his hand. The potato and the needle were gone!

Oh, I lost it in the bushes, he thought. I'll have to go find it. He went back as fast as he could, but he could not find the serviceberry bush. Here are those bracken, and here was where I came out to the trail again, but where is the bush? What shall I do?

He ran down the trail as fast as he could and told his mother. Mrs. Chitwood was alarmed.

"Oh, Jimmy!" she exclaimed. "To think it had to be lost when we had it. Well, we'll just have to find it. Go tell your father."

Jimmy ran to the edge of the clearing where his father and some other men were trimming logs. When Jimmy told what he had done, the men stuck their axes into the logs and went with Jimmy. "We'll have to help, too," they said.

The men and Jimmy went to the cabin. Mrs. Chitwood had sent word to the other neighbors, and they all went up onto the trail where Jimmy thought he had seen the bears.

They looked for bear tracks and found one or two, but the earth was dry. They all looked for the serviceberry bush Jimmy had hidden under, but there were many serviceberry bushes, and where was that one?

Everyone was worried, but no one scolded Jimmy except his sister. She was ten, and she said, "You won't be a good woodsman if you can't even remember landmarks. Don't you know you should always have landmarks?"

Jimmy was white and tearful, but he tried to show his mother exactly where he had been. After a while, he said, "I know there was a stump under the bush. A funny stump."

All the men and women, and children, too, began looking for a red raveling near a stump under a serviceberry bush.

Suddenly Jimmy left the others. He said nothing but walked through a bramble of bracken. When he came out, he went straight to his mother and handed her the potato with the red raveling hanging from it.

"It was by the stump," he said.

"Why, Jimmy," replied his mother, "you are a woodsman, and a reliable boy, to find what you lost. Give it to Grandmother Drain. Quick! Before you lose it again."

Everyone, and that was about twenty-five people, came together to share the joy of finding the needle. Then the men went back to trimming logs, the women went home to get their suppers, and the children went back to their play.

The darning needle was found, and it was kept all that summer and into the fall, but one day when Grandmother Drain was sewing, the head of the needle broke off, and all the women had to make neat piles of clothing to be mended, hoping that before long, someone would come from Fort Vancouver or the East with a needle. Each time women were together they talked of their sewing and hoped that another needle would soon be provided.

One day, about Thanksgiving time, a peddler with a mule came over the pass and down through the canyon. The children playing school on some logs saw him and ran to tell their mothers a visitor was coming.

The mothers, one by one, hurried to see the goods the peddler had brought and to hear news of people to the east. Several hurried to buy combs. One bought a china doll's head. Two women enthusiastically bought dress goods before they thought of needles and thread to sew it with.

Then one of the mothers said, "Oh, do you have any needles? We'll have to have a needle."

"Oh," said Mrs. Chitwood, "how could we forget when it is the one thing we need most—a good needle with a large eye! We need one at least, now that Grandmother Drain's needle is broken." Mrs. Chitwood told the story of the lost darning needle, glancing occasionally at Jimmy who was stroking the mule's neck and pretending not to notice.

Those standing around talked, too, and the peddler listened. Then he reached into his inside pocket.

"My people do not celebrate Christmas," he said, "but I suppose you good people will soon be having a holiday with presents. Are you going to give any presents, sonny?" asked the peddler.

Jimmy looked up quickly. "Oh, yes, sir, that is, I guess I will."

"Well," said the kind-faced man, "suppose you and I give the ladies of Pass Creek Canyon each a Christmas present right now, shall we?"

Jimmy looked puzzled. The peddler opened the thin package he had taken from his pocket. "Here are some darning needles, all I have, but I believe there will be enough for every family in the canyon to have one."

No one said anything for a moment, then there was a gasp of astonishment. The women smiled to each other, "He's a good man."

The peddler and Jimmy passed out the needles to those gathered around, and the next day Jimmy delivered the rest of the needles up and down the canyon.

The peddler left, and no one saw him again for many months, but that was just the first of many kindnesses shown the women in Pass Creek Canyon by Aaron Meier who later founded the store of Meier and Frank in Portland.

The peddler Aaron Meier, born in Germany in 1831, came to America at age twenty-four to work in the store belonging to his two older brothers in the California gold fields. Part of his job was to make the long trips peddling their wares through the Oregon Territory as far north as the Columbia River. He carried his pack on his back as he walked the difficult terrain of the Cascade Mountains.

After two years of this exhausting work, he decided to open his own store in Portland in 1857. Over the years, working with his wife, Jeannette Hirsch, and his son-in-law, Sigmund Frank, he developed Meier and Frank Company into one of America's great family-owned department stores.

Meier and Frank used the darning needle story in a full-page ad in *The Oregonian,* the state's main newspaper, on January 1, 1967. The headline read "Have you ever heard the story of 'The Potato and the Darning Needle'?" At the end of the story was an invitation for all to come into Meier and Frank's Fabric Center to receive a complimentary needle.[14]

this has been a tradition with us at Meier & Frank since Aaron Meier's
e have for 109 years.

We still want every woman to have a darning
needle of her own. Come into our Fabric Center
at any one of our three stores Tuesday and get yours, free.

account written by Mr. Howard M. Corning in the book "With Her Own Wi

Meier and Frank advertisement

APPENDIX C *Preserving the Treasures*

THE MAJORITY OF THE QUILTS IN THIS STUDY are housed in museums and historical societies throughout the country. Without the dedication and interest of their staffs and volunteers, this book and the accompanying exhibition would not be a part of the Oregon Trail celebration.

The role of these public and private institutions has been defined in three ways: to collect and preserve artifacts of the past, to interpret these in exhibits and activities, and to provide an educational outreach to the community. Thus they are vital in preserving and interpreting our nation's heritage and are deserving of our support and interest. We can also assist in their mission. Because they have shared their resources, I will be able to provide them with additional information about their quilt collections.

It is important for would-be donors and those interested in preserving the heritage of the past to understand how these organizations work. To collect and preserve artifacts of the past, a society usually works within a clearly defined territory of time and place, seeking to identify and gather the materials that reflect the heritage of its location. In the past, a museum has been inclined to take all objects brought to its door. In this day of limited financial resources, narrowly defined territories within the mission statement determine exactly which artifacts should be in its collection.

Once the materials are collected, it is important to inventory and register each of the collection's objects to be able to access them when needed and to know what is available. In the case of quilts, this means carefully recording the physical description of each item by noting such things as size, date, fabric content, construction technique and condition. It has been a joy to work with such large historical societies as the Southern Oregon Historical Society in Medford where, in addition to a supportive staff, a photo of each quilt was attached to the accession card. Outstanding examples of private institutions are the museum houses administered by the Oregon Society of the Daughters of the American Revolution, especially the Schminck Museum in Lakeview. The small bungalow houses the lifetime collections of two generations of the James and Elizabeth Currier Foster family. For material culture people, it's a bonanza!

With quilts, it is becoming increasingly important to provide information about the maker, who she was, when and where she lived, and any other important information that would enhance the quilt's interpretation, as has been done in this study.

A further dimension of this gathering of resources is the need to provide proper storage space for the objects. A wide range of solutions is possible, depending on financial resources, and can include a sophisticated, climatically controlled environment or simply shelves out of direct sunlight and free of dust.

For someone considering donating a quilt, it is appropriate to ask questions about each of these matters and to provide as much information as possible to accompany the artifact.

In interpreting the artifacts in exhibits and providing activities to enrich the community's understanding, the focus is usually on an activity or a place or time relevant to the object. For instance, at a quilting demonstration, people are invited to add stitches to a new quilt being made. A quilt exhibition can focus on a certain theme, as does the traveling show accompanying this book.

If a privately owned quilt would complement an exhibition, it is considered a very generous offer to make it available on loan. Several of the quilts of this project are privately owned. All add information to the themes, and they greatly enrich the project.

The educational outreach of the museum or historical society can be achieved through programs, lectures, or publications geared to different age groups within the community. These may be the work of staff personnel or other educators interested in teaching the public about its past history and using a museum's collection of census records, public and personal histories, maps, photographs, and newspapers. The extensive collections of the Oregon Historical Society, available in both artifacts and supporting research materials, add interesting dimensions to the understanding of Oregon's history.

This educational outreach can also take place through individual research by interested people wanting to know more about their own history. For instance, a number of people in Oregon will be seeking to validate the stories they have heard about their own families' experience on the Oregon Trail. As each family's anniversary occurs during the next thirty years, many questions will be addressed to the staffs of museums and historical societies and their resources investigated.

As demonstrated by this research, the more complete the material found, the more interesting and valuable the quilt became. It is vitally important, then, to provide as much documentation as possible when making a donation to a museum. The basic information should include who, what, when, where, why, and how. Then any additional materials in the form of letters, pictures, quilt construction materials, and sewing items that would add to the quilt's interpretation should be included. In addition it would be helpful to include a bibliography of sources, a list of family descendants, or other notations. When an item is donated, it receives a number and an accession sheet that is used to record all this information, sometimes accompanied by a file folder to hold extra materials.

In deciding to make a donation of a family treasure, there are several important guidelines. One is to choose the best possible location for the object. After gathering as much information as possible about the quilt, consider various museums where it might be placed in order to determine the most appropriate disposition. Knowing when and where a quilt was made or used, and learning the museum's mission statement about its territory, its goals, and its existing quilt collection can help one make a comfortable decision. If a quilt was made in the Midwest in a particular county and state, a location related to its origin might be found. If a museum already has a number of quilts of a particular kind or era, it may not be interested in receiving another. If a museum's focus is on farm equipment rather than textiles, it is not an appropriate choice for your quilt. By being patient and carefully evaluating the options, eventually the right museum will be found.

Even if a donation is not being considered, it is a good idea to organize information about it at home so other family members will be able to learn and appreciate more of their own history. It also helps them if a suggestion is made regarding a future permanent location for a quilt or other artifacts.

As these public and private institutions have shared so generously with me, I encourage you to visit them and support their work. A list of locations and directions follows.

OREGON HISTORICAL SOCIETIES AND MUSEUMS

Old Aurora Colony Museum
  P. O. Box 202
  Aurora, OR 97002
  (503) 678-5754
  I-5, Exit 278

Coos Country Historical
  Museum
  1220 Sherman
  North Bend, OR 97459
  (503) 756-6320
  Simpson Park

Crook County Historical Society
  Bowman Museum
  246 North Main Street
  Prineville, OR 97754
  (503) 447-3715
  Downtown Prineville

Douglas County Museum of
  History
  P. O. Box 1550
  Roseburg, OR 97470
  (503) 440-4507
  I-5, Exit 123

High Desert Museum
59800 South Highway 97
Bend, OR 97702-4754
(503) 382-4754

Horner Museum
Gill Coliseum Lower-1
Oregon State University
Corvallis, OR 97331-4104
(503) 754-2951

Junction City Historical Museum
655 Holly Street
Junction City, OR 97448
One block east of Highway 99

Klamath County Museum
1451 Main Street
Klamath Falls, OR 97601
(503) 883-4208

Lane County Historical Museum
740 West 13 Street
Eugene, OR 97402
(503) 687-4239
Lane County Fairgrounds
I-5, Exit 194 West
Follow signs Fairgrounds/
Jefferson

Lincoln County Historical
Society
545 Southwest 9th Street
Newport, OR 97365
(503) 265-7509
1 block east of Highway 101
between Alder and Fall

Molalla Area Historical Society
Dibble House
P. O. Box 828
Molalla, OR 97038
(503) 829-8637

Oregon Historical Society
1230 Southwest Park Avenue
Portland, OR 97205
(503) 222-1741
Southwest Broadway and
Jefferson

DAR Pioneer Mother's
Memorial Cabin
Champoeg State Park
8035 Champoeg Road NE,
St Paul, OR
(503) 633-2237
I-5, Exit 278

Schminck Memorial DAR
Museum
128 South E Street
Lakeview, OR 97630
(503) 947-3134
One block east of Highway
495

Southern Oregon Historical
Society
106 North Central Avenue
Medford, OR 97501
(503) 773-6536
Downtown Medford

Washington County Museum
17677 Northwest Springville
Road
Portland, OR 97229
(503) 645-5353
On the Rock Creek Campus
of Portland Community
College
Highway 26 West

Umatilla County Historical
Society
P. O. Box 253
Pendleton, OR 97801
(503) 276-0012
Old Railroad Depot
Downtown Pendleton

Yamhill County Historical
Museum
P. O. Box 484
Lafayette, OR 97127
Old Church
6th and Market

OTHER MUSEUMS AND
HISTORICAL SOCIETIES

Washington, D.C.
DAR Museum
1776 D Street
Washington, DC 20006
(202) 879-3241

National Museum of
American History
Smithsonian Institution
Washington, DC 20560
(202) 357-1300

Washington

Eastern Washington
Historical Society
Cheney Cowles Museum
West 2316 First Avenue
Spokane, WA 99204
(509) 456-3931

Museum of History and
Industry
2700 24th Avenue East
Seattle, WA 98112
(206) 324-1125

NOTES

Preface

1. Lillian Schlissel, *Women's Diaries of the Westward Journey* (New York: Schocken Books, 1982), 10.

2. Ibid., 155.

3. Lillian Schlissel, Byrd Gibbens, and Elizabeth Hampsten, *Far from Home, Families of the Westward Journey* (New York: Schocken Books, 1989), 238–41.

4. Rachel Maines, "Textiles as History." In *American Quilts, A Handmade Legacy,* edited by Thomas Frye (Oakland, California: Oakland Museum of Art, 1981), 41.

Introduction

1. Lenore Gale Barette, *Christmas in Oregon Territory in 1853.* In Glenn Mason, *A Piece of the Old Tent of 1853* (Eugene, Oregon: Lane County Historical Museum, 1976), 27.

2. Lydia Louisa Whittemore Hutchins, Sampler. Collection of Margaret McNeill Fowler, Ithaca, New York.

3. Elaine Hedges, "The 19th-Century Diarist and Her Quilts." In Frye, *American Quilts,* 60.

4. Anne Hyde, "The Significance of Perception and Interpretation in the History of the American West." Paper presented at the National Endowment for the Humanities Research Conference, Utah State University, Logan, Utah, July 1992.

5. Julie Roy Jeffrey, *Frontier Women, The Trans-Mississippi West 1840–1880* (New York: Hill and Wang, 1979), 87.

Part One: 1840 to 1850

1. Joseph Ware, *The Emigrant's Guide to California.* Quoted in *The Emigrant's Guide to New Mexico, California, and Oregon Giving the Different Overland and Sea Routes Compiled from Reliable Authorities* (New York: J. Disturnell, 1849).

2. Redpath and Hinton, *Hand-book to Kansas Territory,* 145; Rudolph B. Marcy, *The Prairie Traveler: A Handbook for Overland Expeditions* (New York: Harper and Brothers, 1859), 40; O. Allen, *Allen's Guide Book and Map to the Gold Fields of Kansas and Nebraska and Great Salt Lake City* (Washington, D.C.: R. A. Walters, 1859), 5–6. Quoted in Barbara

Brackman, "Quilts on the Kansas Frontier," *Kansas History, a Journal of the Central Plains,* volume 13, number 1 (Spring 1990), 19.

3. John Clark, 1852. In Merle Mattes, *The Great Platte River Road* (Nebraska State Historical Society, 1969), volume 25, 61: "The elephant was the popular symbol of the Great Adventure, all the wonder and the glory and the shivering thrill of the plunge into the ocean of prairie and plains. . . . It was the poetic imagery of all the deadly perils that threatened a westering emigrant."

4. Catherine Haun, *A Woman's Trip Across the Plains in 1849.* In Jeffrey, *Frontier Women,* 41.

5. Charlotte Stearns Pengra, Diary, 1853. In Schlissel, *Women's Diaries,* 81.

6. Pete Peterson, *Our Wagon Train Is Lost* (Eugene, Oregon: New American Gothic, 1975), 20.

7. Jeffrey, *Frontier Women,* 45.

8. Winifred McKenzie, "Noah Franklin Lieuallen 1839–1876," Lieuallen Family Papers. Collection of Gilberta Lieuallen, Adams, Oregon.

9. Amelia Peck, *American Quilts and Coverlets in the Metropolitan Museum of Art* (New York: Metropolitan Museum of Art, 1990), 180–81.

10. Barbara Brackman, telephone conversation with author, June 1992.

11. Rachel Maines, "Paradigms of Scarcity and Abundance: The Quilt as an Artifact of the Industrial Revolution," *Heart of Pennsylvania Symposium Papers* (Lewisburg, Pennsylvania: Oral Traditions Project, 1986), 86. In Brackman, *Clues in the Calico* (McLean, Virginia: EPM Publications, 1989), 113.

12. Virginia Churchill Bath, *Needlework in America* (New York: Viking Press, 1979), 135–47.

13. Fred Scoggin, letter to the author, June 1992.

14. Ruby Lacy, *Oregon Territory 1850 Census* (Self-published, 1984), 73.

15. Documentation File 848, Lane County Historical Museum, Eugene, Oregon.

16. Brackman, *Clues,* 69.

17. Perkins Family Papers, Yamhill County Historical Museum, Lafayette, Oregon.

18. Schminck Scrapbook Number 7. Schminck Memorial Museum, Lakeview Oregon, 13.

19. Rita Adroska, *Natural Dyes and Home Dying*

(New York: Dover, 1971), 30.

20. Brackman, *Clues*, 66–70.

21. Elias Buell, "This Is a True Copy of the Genealogical Account of the Buells, Which Was Written by Elias Buell in 1870." In Mary Fletcher, *History of Polk County* (Polk County, Oregon: Polk County Historical Society, 1987), 70.

22. JoAnn L. Wiss, letter to the author, August 3, 1992.

23. Wright Family History. Collection of Bertha Nolan, Milwaukie, Oregon.

24. Gail McCormick, "Area's First Settler Struck Down by Smallpox," *Everything's Fine-o in Mulino!* (Mulino, Oregon: Self-published), volume 2, number 4.

25. Mabel Glover Root, "Family History of the Oregon Pioneer Families of Philip Glover and John H. Palmer." Unpublished manuscript in the collection of Louise Godfrey (Portland, Oregon), 54.

26. Ibid., 54.

27. Barbara Brackman, *An Encyclopedia of Pieced Quilt Patterns* (Lawrence, Kansas: Prairie Flower Publishing, 1984), number 3772.

28. Lenice Bacon, *American Patchwork Quilts* (New York: Bonanza Books, 1973), 16.

29. Nettie Spencer, "Lucinda Cox." In *With Her Own Wings*, edited by Helen Krebs Smith (Portland, Oregon: Fine Arts Department of Portland, Oregon, Federation of Women's Organizations, 1948), 106–08.

Part Two: 1851 to 1855

1. Gloria Lathrop, "Introduction." In Jean Ray Laury, *Ho for California* (New York: E. P. Dutton, 1990), 15.

2. "Dr. T., 1849." In Ingvard Eide, *Oregon Trail* (Chicago: Rand McNally, 1972), 112–13.

3. James Madison Powell, *Powell Family History* (Portland, Oregon: Design Printing, 1977), 35–36.

4. Dan Stebbins, wheelwright and historian at Wyoming Territorial Prison, conversation with author, August 1992.

5. Jeffrey, *Frontier Woman*, 43.

6. Violet Mumford, *The Royal Way West*, volume 2 (Baltimore: Gateway Press, 1988), 128–35.

7. Starrs Riggs Family Papers, Manuscript File number 2637, Oregon Historical Society, Portland, Oregon.

8. John Bunyan, *Pilgrim's Progress*. In Myron and Patsy Orlofsky, *Quilts in America* (New York: McGraw-Hill, 1974), 265.

9. George H. Greer, "The James Greer Family," Polk County Pioneer Sketches, *Polk County Observer*, 1929, 34–35.

10. Accession File 705, Lane County Historical Museum, Eugene, Oregon.

11. Joseph Gaston, *The Centennial History of Oregon 1811–1912*, volume 2 (S. J. Clarke Publishing, 1911), 249.

12. George W. Riddle, *History of Early Days in Oregon* (Riddle, Oregon: The Riddle Enterprise, 1920), 17.

13. Elly Sienkiewicz, *Spoken Without a Word* (Self-published, 1983), 45.

14. A. C. Seely Papers, Douglas County Museum of History and Natural History, Roseburg, Oregon.

15. Riddle, *Early Days*, 41.

16. *Genealogical Material in Oregon Donation Land Claims* (Portland, Oregon: Genealogical Forum, 1957), volume II, 58.

17. Kevin Mittge, *The Robbins and Herren Families of the Pacific Northwest* (Kirkland, Washington: Self-published, 1988), 12.

18. Brackman, *Encyclopedia*, number 1963.

19. Ibid., 61.

20. Wanita Propst Haugen, interview with author, Albany, Oregon, May 1992.

21. Sienkiewicz, *Spoken Without a Word*, 49.

22. Powell, *Powell Family History*, 310.

23. Pat Ferrero, Elaine Hedges, and Julie Silber, *Hearts and Hands* (San Francisco: Quilt Digest Press, 1987), 18.

24. "The Dibbles and the Dibble House 1856–1859." Collection of Gena Cline, Molalla Area Historical Society, Molalla, Oregon.

25. Clark Will, "Colony Mothers Help Write Colony History." Collection of the Aurora Colony Historical Society, Aurora, Oregon.

26. "1985 Aurora Colony Quilt Show." Collection of the Aurora Colony Historical Society, Aurora, Oregon.

27. Hazelton Family Papers, Lane County Historical Museum Archives, Eugene, Oregon.

28. Work Sheet 2192.1, Eastern Washington Historical Society, Spokane, Washington.

29. Ruth Stoller, letter to the author, July 1992.

30. Nancy Tuckhorn, associate curator, DAR Museum, letter to the author, July 1992.

31. Brackman, *Encyclopedia*, number 1462.

32. Brackman, *Clues*, 91–92.

33. "The Dibbles . . . 1856–1859."

34. Henry E. Morris, "Eliam Morris Family History 1811–1958," *Champoeg Pioneer*, volume 2, number 30, July 1958, 2.

35. Quilt number 1721, Oregon Historical Society, Portland, Oregon.

36. Abigail Scott Duniway, "Editorial Correspondence," *New Northwest*, July 15, 1880. In Ruth Barnes Moynihan, *Rebel for Rights* (New Haven: Yale University Press, 1985), 153.

37. Letter from Aunt Etty (Harriet) to Clyde

Duniway, March 24, 1925, Duniway Papers. In Moynihan, Ibid., 31.

38. Abigail Scott Duniway, *From the West to the West: Across the Plains to Oregon* (Chicago: A. C. McClurg, 1905), 147. In Moynihan, Ibid., xiii.

39. Grace Jane Simpson Skeeters, "The Life of Mrs. Grace Jane Skeeters," Southern Oregon Historical Society Archives, Medford, Oregon.

40. Penny McMorris, *Crazy Quilts* (New York: Dutton, 1986), 12.

Part Three: 1856 to 1870

1. Mrs. Elizabeth Currier Foster, interview in 1914 (no documentation). Collection of the Schminck Museum, Lakeview, Oregon.

2. Riddle, *Early Days,* 29.

3. Larry Carten, "Pioneers Found Blue Mountains Main Obstacle on Oregon Trail," *Oregon Journal,* February 12, 1956.

4. Ibid., 10.

5. William Denison Lyman, *Old Walla Walla County* (Chicago: S. J. Clarke Publishing Company, 1918), 609–10.

6. Barbara Brackman, "Quilts on the Kansas Frontier," *Kansas History,* volume 13, number 1 (Spring 1990), 76.

7. "Diary of Nathaniel Myer." In Edward Ham, "Journey into Southern Oregon: Diary of a Pennsylvania Dutchman," *Oregon Historical Quarterly* (September 1959), 385–86.

8. Andrew S. McClure, Journal 1853. In Peterson, *Wagon Train,* 21.

9. Pengra, Diary 1853. In Schlissel, *Women's Diaries,* 99.

10. John Boardman, 1843. In Eide, *Oregon Trail,* 191.

11. E. L. Meyers, "Barlow Road," unpublished manuscript, Portland, Oregon Historical Society, 5.

12. Mildred Baker Burcham, "Our Knight Heritage," Aurora Colony Historical Society, Aurora, Oregon, 3.

13. Settlement Records 1878, Aurora Colony Historical Society, Aurora, Oregon, 49.

14. Stauffer Family Papers. Collection of Vera Yoder, Woodburn, Oregon.

15. Sienkiewicz, *Spoken Without a Word,* 39.

16. Goddard and Robinson Family History. Collection of Bonnie Furry, Medford, Oregon; Lida Childers, telephone conversation with author, August 1992.

17. Mabel Lieuallen Wagner, *Water from the Spring,* unpublished manuscript. Collection of Gilberta Lieuallen, Adams, Oregon.

18. Bettina Havig, *Missouri Heritage Quilts* (Padu-

cah, Kentucky: American Quilters Society, 1986), 62–63.

19. Brackman, *Encyclopedia,* number 3842.

20. Brackman, *Calico,* 66–70.

21. Lena Lieuallen and Mabel Lieuallen Wagner, "Memories of Grandpa and Grandma Lieuallen," unpublished manuscript collection of Gilberta Lieuallen, Athena, Oregon.

22. Lena Lieuallen, family history notes. Collection of Gilberta Lieuallen, Adams, Oregon.

23. Mrs. George Blankenship, *Early History of Thurston County, Washington, Together with Biographies and Reminiscences of Those Identified with Pioneer Days* (Olympia, Washington: publisher unknown, 1914), 214.

24. Barbara Brackman, letter to the author, July 15, 1992.

25. Helen Barrett Woodroofe, "Quilt Recalls a Strong, Good Woman," *The Callaway Journal* (volume 8, 1983), 62.

26. Bryan Family History. In Joyce Gross, *Quilts of the West,* Exhibition Catalog, Mill Valley, California, 9.

27. Brackman, *Encyclopedia,* number 3536.

28. Documentation File number 476, Lane County Historical Museum, Eugene, Oregon.

29. Goddard and Robison Family History. Collection of Bonnie Furry, Medford, Oregon.

30. Ruth Finley, *Old Patchwork Quilts and the Women Who Made Them* (Newton Center, Massachusetts: Charles Branford, 1957), 93.

31. Clark Will, *The Story of Old Aurora in Pictures and Prose 1856–1883* (Self-published, 1972), 24.

32. Patrick Harris, interview with the author, July 1992.

Part Four: Those Who Wait

1. Note attached to quilt by Robert S. Bell, M. D.

2. *Genealogical Material in Oregon Donation Land Claim,* Genealogical Forum, 1957, volume II, number 5022.

3. Francis Bell Mezger, Scottsdale, Arizona. Telephone conversation with author, May 1992.

4. Suellen Meyer, "Pine Tree Quilts," *The Quilt Digest* (San Francisco: The Quilt Digest Press, 1986), 14.

5. Bipi Soukey, "Ashland's Original Granddaughter," *Ashland Plaza,* May 1978.

6. Kay Atwood, *Mill Creek Journal, Ashland, Oregon 1850–1860* (Ashland, Oregon: Self-published, 1987), 31.

7. Soukey, *Ashland Plaza.*

Postlude
1. The Reverend George H. Atkinson, "Journal 1847." In Eide, *Oregon Trail*, 219.
2. Jeffrey, *Frontier Women*, xv.
3. Charles Nordhoff, *The Communistic Societies of the United States* (New York: Dover, 1966), 305–20.
4. Christopher Carlson, "The Rural Family in the 19th Century: A Case Study in Oregon's Willamette Valley" (Ph.D. dissertation, University of Oregon, 1980), 186–93.
5. Miranda Bayley Smith, "Kidnapped by Indians, A Pioneer's Story." Manuscript File, Yamhill County Historical Museum, Lafayette, Oregon.
6. Brett Harvey Vuolo, "Pioneer Diaries: The Untold Story of the West, *MS*, May 1975, 34. In C. Kurt Dewhurst, Betty MacDowell, and Marsha MacDowell, *Artists in Aprons: Folk Art by American Women* (New York: Dutton, 1979), 110.
7. "Mrs. Dr. Owens-Adair," *History of the Pacific Northwest: Oregon and Washington* (Portland: North Pacific History Company, n.d.), 502–06.

Appendixes
1. Sienkiewicz, *Spoken Without a Word*, 31–49.
2. John H. Clark, "Overland to the Gold Fields of California in 1852," Louise Berry, ed., *Kansas Historical Quarterly, 11* (August 1942), 229. In Sandra Myres, *Westering Women and the Frontier Experience 1800–1915* (Albuquerque, New Mexico: University of New Mexico Press, 1982), 101.
3. Brackman, *Encyclopedia*, 170–72.

4. Gunn, Virginia, "Romance and Reality: A Century in Quilt Scholarship 1890–1990." Paper presented as part of panel, Directions in Quilt Scholarship, Bibliography Conference (Louisville, Kentucky), February 6–8, 1992.
5. See Ruth Finley, *Old Patchwork Quilts and the Women Who Made Them* (Newton Centre, Massachusetts: Charles Branford, 1929), 130–31; Carrie Hall and Rosa Kretzinger, *The Romance of the Patchwork Quilt in America* (New York: Bonanza Books, 1935), 74.
6. Tabitha Brown, letter to brother and sister, August 1854. In *Pacific University Bulletin*, 32, December 1936.
7. Elizabeth Geer, Journal. In Eide, *Oregon Trail*, 219–20.
8. Eleanor Allen, *Canvas Caravans* (Portland, Oregon: Binford and Mort, 1946), 116–23.
9. Leah Collins Menefee and Lowell Tiller, "Cutoff Fever," *Oregon Historical Quarterly* (September 1977), 213.
10. Pete Peterson, *Our Wagon Train Is Lost*, 15.
11. Ibid., 28–29.
12. Catherine Leonard Jones. Letter to Mrs. C. H. Dye, November 12, 1903. Collection of Patricia Erlandson, Sunriver, Oregon.
13. John Bruce Bell, letter to friend Mary, May 21, 1855. In the collection of Mrs. Robert S. Bell.
14. Lois Allen Stewart, letter to the author, June 1992.

GLOSSARY

Appliqué: a category of quilts constructed by laying one fabric on top of another and stitching the two together.

Bed Rug: a twentieth-century term used to define the rug used on a bed in the seventeenth and eighteenth centuries when it was referred to as a rug. It was a heavily embroidered or hooked wool-based covering. Surface designs from these were used as whole cloth quilt designs.

Binding: the finish to the raw edge of the quilt, usually a strip of straight or bias fabric.

Block: the unit or section of the quilt made by joining fabric pieces or appliquéing them together. It is often the unit of design of the quilt pattern.

Border: the band of fabric stitched to the edge of the top to give the extra needed width or length.

Cholera: a rapidly fatal disease that could strike and kill within hours of the first symptoms, usually diarrhea, then followed by sore throat, abdominal pains, leg cramps, chills, fever and ending with vomiting, the worst and final symptom. If a dose of medicine such as laudanum were available early enough, recovery was possible.

Crazy Quilt: a style of quilt made in the last half of the nineteenth century where irregular shapes of fabric are stitched together and embellished with embroidery stitches.

Design: the overall organization of the quilt, or a specific pattern.

Drawnwork: embroidery done on an area where the threads have been withdrawn in one direction.

Elbow or Fan Quilting: the style of quilting lines made using the elbow as a fulcrum for marking the lines on the quilt top. A series of marks are made, evenly spaced on a surface. Then the elbow is placed on a mark and an arc is made by marking the line for quilting by swinging the hand in an arc. This was a very effective and fast method of marking quilt lines if one was not quilting a separate motif in each block or outlining each design.

Indigo-Blue: a color produced by a multi-process. First, a vat process of fermentation gets the dye liquid from the Indigofera plant. Then a process of oxidation to color the fabric by soaking up the liquid and exposing it to air is followed.

Indigo-Blue and White Fabric: colorfast textiles featuring interesting design elements mass produced and readily available to quiltmakers in the States with the development of the textile industry in America, including improved dying and printing processes.

Medallion: a quilt with a large central motif on the top surrounded by additional designs and/or borders.

Mourning Prints: the fine black lines and figures printed close enough on a white background fabric to appear gray. They were called this in the mail-order catalogs of the late nineteenth century.

Nooning: the break taken at mid-day during the journey for food and rest for people and animals.

On Point: the arrangement of quilt blocks with the corners touching the baseline and one another.

Pieced: the category of quilts constructed by joining the edges of fabrics together to make the top, usually in a geometric pattern.

Quilt: two layers of fabric placed with a batting between stitched or tied together, a textile sandwich.

Rainbow Print: the fabric produced by varying the shades of color on the printing press roller to produce a rainbow of colors or different intensities of the same color. The use in quilts was popular between 1820 and 1860.

Roller Print Fabric: a revolutionary step in textile production in the late 1700s where the flat plate was wrapped around a roller on the printing press, allowing the continuous printing of fabric. The effect was immediate, producing significantly more and better quality printed fabrics by the 1830s.

Set: the arrangement of the quilt blocks or squares.

Template: the pattern piece followed in cutting the fabric for a design.

Tufted Candlewicking: the process of using a thick thread of several strands of wicking to make the loops of the running stitch. Using a stick or wire as gauge, these stitches are left about one quarter of an inch in height above the surface of the cloth instead of drawing the thread down to the surface. These loops are cut to create a tuft, or pile. More often there is a combination of embroidery, uncut candlewicking, and tufted pile. The uncut candlewicking gives greater clarity to the design while the tufted pile gives a greater richness.*

White Work: a quilt top of all white fabric with white embroidery or quilting.

Whole Cloth: a quilt top made of one fabric, either a solid piece or several stitched together.

*Virginia Bath, *Needlework in America*, Viking Press, 1979, pp. 144–145

BIBLIOGRAPHY

QUILTS AND QUILT HISTORY

Many excellent quilt books are available today for research and study of quiltmakers and their art. This bibliography, however, limits itself to those who made a direct contribution to the research for this volume on the quilts and quiltmakers of the Oregon Trail.

Adroska, Rita. *Natural Dyes and Home Dying*. New York: Dover, 1971.

Bacon, Lenice. *American Patchwork Quilts*. New York: Bonanza Books, 1973.

Bath, Virginia Churchill. *Needlework in America*. New York: Viking Press, 1979.

Better Homes and Gardens. *American Heritage Quilts*. Des Moines, Iowa: Meredith Corporation, 1991.

Bowman, Doris. *The Smithsonian Treasury American Quilts*. Washington, D.C.: Smithsonian Institution, 1991.

Brackman, Barbara. *An Encyclopedia of Pieced Quilt Patterns*. Lawrence, Kansas: Prairie Flower Publishing, 1984.

————. *Clues in the Calico: A Guide to Identifying and Dating Antique Quilts*. McLean, Virginia: EPM Publications, 1989.

Bresenhan, Karoline Patterson, and Nancy O'Bryant Puentes. *Lone Stars: A Legacy of Texas Quilts, 1836–1936*. Austin, Texas: University of Texas, 1986.

Clark, Ricky, George Knepper, and Ellice Ronsheim. *Quilts in Community: Ohio's Traditions*. Nashville, Tennessee: Rutledge Hill Press, 1991.

Dewhurst, C. Kurt, Betty MacDowell, and Marsha MacDowell. *Artists in Aprons: Folk Art by American Women*. New York: E. P. Dutton, 1979.

Ferrero, Pat, Elaine Hedges, and Julie Silber. *Hearts and Hands: The Influence of Women and Quilts on American Society*. San Francisco, California: Quilt Digest Press, 1987.

Frye, Thomas, ed. *American Quilts, A Handmade Legacy*. Oakland, California: Museum of Art, 1981.

Finley, Ruth. *Old Patchwork Quilts and the Women Who Made Them*. Newton Center, Massachusetts: Charles Branford, 1929.

Gross, Joyce. *Quilts of the West*. Mill Valley, California: Self-published, 1976.

Hall, Carrie, and Rose Kretsinger. *The Romance of the Patchwork Quilt in America*. New York: Bonanza Books, 1935.

Havig, Betina. *Missouri Heritage Quilts*. Paducah, Kentucky: American Quilters' Society, 1985.

Jenkins, Susan, and Linda Seward. *The American Quilt Story*. Emmaus, Pennsylvania: Rodale Press, 1991.

Kimball, Jeana. *Red and Green: An Appliqué Tradition*. Bothell, Washington: A Patchwork Place, 1990.

Lasansky, Jeannette. *In the Heart of Pennsylvania: 19th & 20th Century Quiltmaking Traditions*. Lewisburg, Pennsylvania: Oral Traditions Project, 1985.

Laury, Jean Ray, and California Heritage Quilt Project. *Ho for California*. New York: E. P. Dutton, 1990.

McMorris, Penny. *Crazy Quilts*. New York: E. P. Dutton, 1986.

Orlofsky, Myron and Patsy. *Quilts in America*. New York: McGraw-Hill, 1974.

Peck, Amelia. *American Quilts and Coverlets in The Metropolitan Museum of Art*. New York: Dutton Studio Books, 1991.

Robertson, Elizabeth. *American Quilts*. Studio Publications, 1948.

Sienkiewicz, Elly. *Spoken Without a Word*. Washington, D.C.: Self-published, 1983.

Stowe, Harriet Beecher. *Minister's Wooing*. New York: Hurst and Company, n.d.

Swan, Susan. *Plain and Fancy: American Women and Their Needlework, 1700–1850*. New York: Holt, Rinehart, and Winston, 1977.

Webster, Marie. *Quilts: Their Story and How to Make Them*. New York: Tudor, 1915.

HISTORICAL BACKGROUND

Books

Allen, Eleanor. *Canvas Caravans*. Portland, Oregon: Binford and Mort, 1946.

Atwood, Kay. *Mill Creek Journal, Ashland Oregon 1850 1860*. Ashland, Oregon: Self-published, 1987.

Blankenship, Mrs. George. *Early History of Thurston County, Washington with Biographies and Reminiscences of Those Identified with Pioneer Days*. Olympia, Washington: no publisher, 1914.

Carlson, Christopher. *The Rural Family in the 19th Century: A Case Study in Oregon's Willamette Valley*. Eugene, Oregon: University of Oregon, 1980.

Eide, Ingvard. *Oregon Trail*. Chicago: Rand McNally, 1972.

Fletcher, Mary. *History of Polk County*. Dallas, Oregon: Polk County Historical Society, 1987.

Gaston, Joseph. *The Centennial History of Oregon 1811–1912*. Volume II. Chicago: S. J. Clarke Publishing, 1911.

Genealogical Material in Oregon Donation Land Claims. Volume II. Portland, Oregon: Genealogical Forum, 1957.

History of Southern Oregon, Portland, Oregon: A. G. Walling, 1884.

Howell, Erle. *Methodism in the Northwest*. Nashville, Tennessee. The Parthenon Press, 1966.

Hyde, Anne. *An American Vision: Far Western Landscape and National Culture, 1820–1920*. New York: New York University Press, 1990.

Jeffrey, Julie Roy. *Frontier Women: The Trans-Mississippi West 1840–1880*. New York: Hill and Wang, 1979.

Lacy, Ruby. *Oregon Territory 1850 Census*. Self-published, 1984.

Lyman, William Denison. *Old Walla Walla County*. Chicago: S. J. Clarke Publishing, 1918.

Mason, Glenn. *A Piece of the Old Tent of 1853*. Eugene, Oregon: Lane County Historical Museum, 1976.

Mattes, Merrill. *The Great Platte River Road*. Lincoln, Nebraska: University of Nebraska Press, 1969.

Mittge, Kevin. *The Robbins and Herren Families of the Pacific Northwest*. Self-published, 1988.

Moynihan, Ruth Barnes. *Rebel for Rights, Abigail Scott Duniway*. New Haven, Connecticut: Yale University Press, 1983.

Mumford, Violet Coe. *The Royal Way West Volume II, Crossing the Plains, 1853*. Baltimore, Maryland: Gateway Press, 1988.

Myres, Sandra. *Westering Women and the Frontier Experience 1800–1915*. Albuquerque, New Mexico: University of New Mexico Press, 1982.

Nordhoff, Charles. *The Communistic Societies of the United States*. New York: Dover, 1966.

Peterson, Pete. *Our Wagon Train Is Lost*. Eugene, Oregon: New American Gothic, 1975.

Polk County Oregon Marriage Records 1849–1879. No publisher, n.d.

Powell, James Madison. *Powell History*. Portland, Oregon: Design Printing, 1977.

Riddle, George W. *History of Early Days in Oregon*. Riddle, Oregon: The Riddle Enterprise, 1920.

Schlissel, Lillian. *Women's Diaries of the Westward Journey*. New York: Schocken, 1982.

Schlissel, Lillian, Byrd Gibbens, and Elizabeth Hampsten. *Far from Home, Families of the Westward Journey*. New York: Schocken, 1989.

Smith, Helen Krebs, ed. *With Her Own Wings*. Portland, Oregon: Oregon Federation of Women's Organizations, 1948.

Will, Clark. *The Story of Old Aurora in Picture and Prose 1856–1883*. Self-published, 1972.

World Atlas. Chicago: Rand McNally, 1968.

Yarnes, Thomas. *A History of Oregon Methodism*. Oregon Methodist Conference Historical Society, n.d.

Articles, Family Histories, Letters, Magazines, Pamphlets, Papers

Albro, Mary Drain. "The Darning Needle Story." Gerry Frank, Salem, Oregon.

Bell Family Papers. National Museum of American History, Smithsonian Institution, Washington, D.C.

Bell, John Bruce. "Letter to Friend Mary, May 21st, 1855." Mrs. Robert S. Bell, Burlington, Iowa.

Brackman, Barbara. "A Chronological Index to Pieced Quilt Patterns 1775–1825," *Uncoverings: The Journal of the American Quilt Study Group*. Edited by Sally Garoutte, 1983.

———. "Quilts on the Kansas Frontier," *Kansas History*. Volume 13, Number 1, Spring 1990.

Brown, Tabitha. "Letter to Brother and Sister, August, 1854," *Pacific University Bulletin*. Volume 32, Number 6, December 1936.

Burcham, Mildred Baker. "Our Knight Heritage." Aurora Colony Historical Society, Aurora, Oregon.

Carten, Larry. "Pioneers Found Blue Mountains Main Obstacle on Oregon Trail," *Oregon Journal*. February 12, 1956.

Clark, Ricky. "Mid-19th Century Album and Friendship Quilts 1860–1920," *Pieced by Mother*. Edited by Jeannette Lasansky. Oral Traditions Project, 1987.

"The Dibbles and the Dibble House 1856–1859." Gena Cline, Mollala, Oregon.

Garoutte, Sally. "Marseilles Quilts and Their Woven Offspring," *Uncoverings: The Journal of the American Quilt Study Group*. Edited by Sally Garoutte, 1982.

Goddard and Robison Family Papers. Bonnie Furry, Medford, Oregon.

Greer, George. "The James Greer Family," *Polk County Pioneer Sketches*. Dallas, Oregon: Polk County Observer, 1929.

Gunn, Virginia. "Romance and Reality: A Century in Quilt Scholarship 1890–1990." Paper presented at the Bibliography Conference, February 1992, Louisville, Kentucky.

Ham, Edward. "Journey into Southern Oregon: Diary of a Pennsylvania Dutchman," *Oregon Historical Quarterly*. Volume 60, Number 3, September 1959.

Hazelton Family Papers. Lane County Historical Museum, Eugene, Oregon.

Helfrich, Devere. "Applegate Trail 1971," *Klamath Echoes*. Number 9.

Hyde, Anne. "The Significance of Perception and Interpretation in the History of the American West." Paper presented at the National Endowment for the Humanities Research Conference. Utah State University, July 1992.

Jones, Catherine Leonard. Letter to Mrs. C. H. Dye, November 12, 1900. Patricia Erlandson, Sunriver, Oregon.

Lieuallen, Lena, and Mabel Lieuallen Wagner. *Memories of Grandpa and Grandma Lieuallen*. Unpublished manuscript. Gilberta Lieuallen, Adams, Oregon.

Madden, Mary. "Textile Diaries: Kansas Quilt Memories," *Kansas History*. Volume 13, Number 1.

McCormick, Gail. *Everything's Fine-O in Mulino!* Volume 2, Number 4. Self-published, Mulino, Oregon.

McKenzie, Winifred. "Noah Franklin Lieuallen 1839–1876." Lieuallen Family Papers, Gilberta Lieuallen, Adams, Oregon.

Menefee, Leah Collins, and Lowell Tiller. "Cutoff Fever," Oregon Historical Quarterly. Volume 78, Number 3, September 1977.

Meyer, Suellen. "Pine Tree Quilts," *The Quilt Digest 4*. Edited by Michael Kile. San Francisco, California: Quilt Digest Press, 1986.

Meyers, E. L. *Barlow Toll Road 1846–1919: The Story of Two from Fort Deposit*. Portland, Oregon: Genealogical Forum, 1972.

Morris, Henry. "Eliam Morris Family History 1811–1958," *Champoeg Pioneer*. Volume 2, Number 30, July 1958.

"1985 Aurora Colony Quilt Show." Aurora Colony Historical Society, Aurora, Oregon.

Osaki, Amy Boyce. "A 'Truly Feminine Employment': Sewing and the Early Nineteenth-Century Woman," *Winterthur Portfolio*. Volume 23, Number 4, 1988.

Perkins Family Papers. Yamhill County Historical Museum, Lafayette, Oregon.

Root, Mabel Glover. *Family History of the Oregon Pioneer Families of Philip Glover and John H. Palmer*. Louise Godfrey, Portland, Oregon.

Schminck Family Papers. Schminck Memorial Museum, Lakeview, Oregon.

Seely, A. C. Family Papers. Douglas County Museum of History and Natural History, Roseburg, Oregon.

"Settlement Records 1878." Aurora Colony Historical Society, Aurora, Oregon.

Skeeters, Grace Jane Simpson. "The Life of Mrs. Grace Jane Simpson Skeeters." Southern Oregon Historical Society Archives, Medford, Oregon.

Smith Family Papers. Yamhill County Historical Museum, Lafayette, Oregon.

Soukey, Bippi. "Ashland's Original Granddaughter," *Ashland Plaza*. May 1978.

Starr-Riggs Family Papers #2637. Oregon Historical Society, Portland, Oregon.

Starr Family Donation, Accession Files 1967 and 1976. Oregon Historical Society, Portland, Oregon.

Stauffer Family Papers. Vera Yoder, Woodburn, Oregon.

Wagner, Mabel Lieuallen. *Water from the Spring*. Unpublished manuscript. Gilberta Lieuallen, Athena, Oregon.

Ware, Joseph. "The Emigrant's Guide to California," *The Emigrant's Guide to New Mexico, California, and Oregon Giving the Different Overland and Sea Routes Compiled from Reliable Authorities*. J. Disturnell, 1849.

Will, Clark. "Colony Mothers Help Write Colony History." Aurora Colony Historical Society, Aurora, Oregon.

Woodroofe, Helen Barrett. "Quilt Recalls a Strong, Good Woman," *The Callaway Journal*. Volume 8, 1983.

Wright Family History. Bertha Nolan, Milwaukie, Oregon.

Map

"The Oregon Trail," Smith Western, 1133 NW Glisan Street, Portland, Oregon, 97209 (503) 227-6101

INDEX